Boris Diekmann

CHIEF
ENERGY
OFFICER

Universal Principles to nurture
a Spirit of Performance

Illustrations by Anu Chacko

RETHINK PRESS

First published in Great Britain in 2019 by
Rethink Press (www.rethinkpress.com)

Praise

'*Chief Energy Officer* is more than a book. It's a beautiful experience. After reading the first few pages, I found myself gravitating to my big comfortable chair, sitting under a warm blanket, and reading while sipping a cup of delicious tea. That's the feeling tone of this wonderful book. It's more like catching up with an old friend than reading a conventional business book. At the same time, the author takes a clear stand for the possibility that we can forge and enjoy truly authentic relationships in business settings. The author has a deep and vast love of people, and he celebrates relationships as a shining gem often hidden in plain sight. *Chief Energy Officer* challenges its readers not just with a new model or framework, but with an entirely new worldview. In this world, organizations and the people who lead them appreciate and nurture the humanity of their people. In this world, leaders understand that high performance doesn't happen despite the "soft skills" of relationships, but because of them.'

Erica Ariel Fox, *New York Times* bestselling author of *Winning From Within: A Breakthrough Method for Leading, Living, and Lasting Change*

'Boris Diekmann has written a seminal book on the insight into transformational change. This is a book every leader needs to read and re-read. The prescient understanding of individual as well as collective need for the application of forgiveness, foresight, deep care, and mindfulness provides necessary wisdom for today's compassionate leader. The dialogical nature of the book pulls the reader into a persuasive narrative rather than the traditional pedantic style of most leadership books and in doing so instructs leaders how the one-to-one nature of transformative change begins at the person to person level. This will be a book that our leaders will be reading and will be living.'

Jennifer Crowell Ferch, Chief Operating Officer for NBC Camps, Academy of Sports Excellence, training thousands of athletes each summer in six countries and over 250 weeks of summer camps

'"We can't solve problems by using the same kind of thinking we used when we created them." said Albert Einstein. Boris Diekmann's seminal *Chief Energy Officer* inspires leaders to look at their role and their organizations through a different dimension – human energy. It provides deep yet hands-on wisdom that has not only proven to be effective in helping managers dealing with tough challenges yet, even more importantly, land their teams and their organizational cultures on higher ground in the process. A must-read for all leaders and management teams.'

Azim Khamisa, Founder and CEO of ANK Enterprises, Speaker, Thought Leader, author of four books including the award-winning *From Murder to Forgiveness* and *The Secrets of the Bulletproof Spirit*; www.azimkhamisa.com

'Written as a conversation between two co-workers, *Chief Energy Officer* contains a goldmine of opportunities for any company, manager or, indeed, individual looking to understand the sources of energy that can unlock greatness in human performance and relationships. The reader is taken on a constant journey of understanding and reflections linked to how the four key energy sources – the heart, the mind, the body and the soul – can influence our own mindset and how conditioning our personal responses can unlock an amazing transformation in culture and the mindset of others. A no-nonsense game changer!'

Brian Murray, Group HR Director of Nomad Foods, UK

'We live in a very exciting time: we all feel we need to redefine how we, Humans, are living on this beautiful planet. It is exciting and scary at the same time. In his book, *Chief Energy Officer*, Boris Diekmann helps us understand how we can shift our mind and better use what is deep inside us to develop healthy organizations to build a better future. Bergson said: 'the future is uncertain because it depends on us'. If many of us are making some steps towards becoming better Chief Energy Officers, we will build a better world.'

Olivier Legrain, CEO IBA, Belgium

'With this book, Boris pioneers the role of leadership as that of transforming energy through four principles or sources that enable us to become our own Chief Energy Officers. Engaging us in "real fiction" dialogue, he focuses our attention on how we can choose inspired leadership as a concrete path to bring purpose and meaning into our lives and work. Readers will find themselves expanding their thoughts and feelings about leadership and business to realize how they can channel the spirit of performance (the energy) in their organizations into experiences of deep meaning.'

Ann L. Clancy, Ph.D., Executive Coach and Organizational Consultant, author of *Appreciative Coaching* and *Pivoting: A Coach's Guide for Igniting Substantial Change*

'An insightful and powerful book, written with a captivating simplicity. We are humans and cannot not feel. It is key to understand how we can awaken positive energy in our organizations. Reading this book has made me become fully aware of the role of my mind, heart, spirit and body. A must-read for those who want to "shift hearts" and achieve results in the workplace.'

Shireen El Khatib, CEO of Majid Al Futtaim – Fashion, Dubai

'*Chief Energy Officer* is a quick read that shows us how the success of the team is so strongly impacted by how true the CEO operates within the circle of energy and then brings all of the team members into that circle. *Chief Energy Officer* is a good read for all levels of leadership who are truly the "CEOs" of their own teams.'

Dennis Litos, CEO of Ingham Regional Medical Center, Lansing MI

To Francesca, Luis and Sophia.

'Thus the task is not to see what nobody
yet has seen, but to think what nobody yet has
thought about that which everybody sees.'

Schopenhauer

Thus the task is not to see what nobody yet has seen, but to see for ourselves what was always there to be seen once we're ready to see.

Contents

Foreword

Boris offers a unique approach to sharing time-tested, healthy high-performance principles in his debut book, *Chief Energy Officer.* As a lifetime learner who consistently challenges the status quo, Boris engages the reader in a conversational journey between two memorable characters, Paul and Maryam, as they explore these principles, inviting the reader to eavesdrop on them. *Chief Energy Officer* shows that anyone can explore and benefit from awakening a deeper understanding of how they can enhance their life effectiveness.

The common experience of casual but meaningful conversations with a friend/mentor is something we are all likely to be able to relate to. Boris points out that profound understandings of how the human experience can evolve can happen in the normal course of day-to-day life, allowing us to become the proverbial 'fly on the wall' to absorb the depth and meaning revealed through the two main characters' conversations. Paul is an insightful mentor who brings out Maryam's curiosity and observations on how she can build more energy and engagement in those around her. As Paul and Maryam exhibit ease and grace throughout the story, we feel that both become our friends.

It has been said that change and evolution in all of us come from the inside out rather than the outside in. In order for Maryam to have the epiphanies she requires for personal growth, she needs to be willing to listen with true curiosity to Paul's insights. Paul by contrast is able to share his understandings through his normal day-to-day existence. This gives all readers the hope that their own insights can come through normal conversations and experiences with others. Boris's approach helps us feel as though we are on the same journey of understanding as Paul and Maryam.

Considering the depth of the principles presented by Boris through his two characters, you may wish to consume the chapters in separate sittings. You can take each lesson discussed by Paul and Maryam, explore it in depth for yourself and engage others in conversations around those ideas. Let your curiosity take over. When you eavesdrop on Paul and Maryam, be willing to let their conversations percolate and sink in.

The principles Boris presents in *Chief Energy Officer* have factored significantly in my own journey as a leader, spouse and parent. Faced with life's challenges that came with acquiring a company from a failing parent company, I could have been consumed with anxiety and fear of failure, while hundreds were counting on me. I was able to see the ephemeral nature of those thoughts, regain my perspective and bring my best to the table. The energy I created encouraged those around me to join my journey to success.

My continuing growth in better understanding the role my thinking plays in my reality led me to engage every one of our employees and clients in their own developmental journey of personal purpose and healthy functioning. This understanding and engagement by all employees led us to become the world's premier organisational culture-shaping company.

Having worked with Fortune 500 CEOs for over twenty-three years, I believe Boris has captured a number of key principles successful leaders consistently employ. Bringing energy is necessary to effect change and growth in people and organisations, so whether you are leading or are a member of a team, developing your grounding in these principles will be core to your success. Enjoy exploring your keys to success by living through the authenticity, meaning, curiosity and resiliency that are presented through the Paul and Maryam conversations.

Jim Hart

Former CEO, Senn Delaney

April 2019

Introduction

'There are two ways of spreading light:
to be the candle or the mirror that reflects it.'

Edith Wharton

'All intelligent thoughts have already been thought;
what is necessary is only to try to think them again.'

Johann Wolfgang von Goethe

T he best way to read this book is to skip the introduction and start with Chapter 1. If you're still reading the intro, then you've probably either chosen to ignore this advice because you find introductions helpful to get some context, or followed my advice and are referring back after having finished the book. Either way, if you're interested in the intention behind the book, then you're in the right place.

Building bridges

This book doesn't contain any idea that hasn't been thought before. In fact, every perspective I've shared throughout this story has already been thought and said, many times, both by people who lived before me and those who are sharing this earth with me right now – people who, in my view, are far more educated, wise and loving than I will ever manage to be. For a long time, this belief stopped me from writing. What could I possibly add?

One of the things that shifted my view and gave birth to the book you're now holding were the conversations I've had over the past ten years or so in my role as consultant, facilitator, coach, colleague, manager, spouse, dad, friend or fellow human being.

One day, after a workshop in Norway, a participant kindly offered to drive me to my nearby hotel. On our way back, he turned to me and said, 'There's a book in you. Do you know that? What stops you from writing?' I felt flattered, of course, yet without further reflection, I explained why this was not my calling. While I can't recall the exact words he used when replying, what he said went along the lines of:

'Boris, that might be true or not. But it's irrelevant. I read a lot myself about what we explored today. I'm interested in the human condition. Yet, you've somehow helped me to better connect with both my own wisdom and that of others. The way you spoke, the questions you asked and the energy you brought to the room resonated with me and enabled me to see what was always there. You've made me connect things that seemed separate before. Something is happening right now. I don't think I'm the only one who you could serve. Think about it.'

That's when he left me standing at the hotel entrance. His name is Paul Sewell.

I started writing three years later, when the opportunity presented itself. During these years, I came to see more clearly that my role is not so much about bringing newness; what gives me life and joy is to build bridges. I love to build bridges between *people and their true selves,* helping them to walk home. I love to build bridges between *people and others*, helping them see greatness in each other beyond their obvious limitations and imperfections. I see a need for building bridges between *ideas and people*, enabling leaders to reconcile and leverage both the more intangible aspects of business, such as thoughts, mindsets, feelings or intuition, and the tangible aspects of business reality such as decisions, policies, technology, organisation, behaviours and financial results. And finally, I get energy from building bridges between *ideas*. While they may use different language, come from different sources and traditions and employ different methods (eg scientific research or contemplation), ideas often point to the same underlying universal truth.

In fact, over the years, when reading books or meeting people sharing their perspectives in the domain of human development, I have become increasingly surprised by the clear connections I could see on the one hand, and the lack of connections being made between the various fields on the other hand. Whether we look at life through the lens of science and applied science, such as biology, psychology, neurology, or physics, or explore insights gained from professional and phenomenological experience – be that in leadership, coaching, sports, education, social work or arts, or we look into the ancient wisdom conveyed to us through religious or spiritual traditions and practices, if we look deeply enough, they point to the same universal truths, and the same mystery. There's a huge opportunity for us not only to keep all doors open, but to connect what started out separately.

In his wonderful book *The Joy of Living*, Buddhist monk Yongey Mingyur Rinpoche describes his early exploration of modern science:

> It was a bit like learning two languages at the same time: Buddhism on the one hand, modern science on the other.

I remember thinking even then that there didn't seem to be much difference between the two.

In his foreword to the same book, Daniel Goleman points out:

We are witnessing an unparalleled episode in the history of science: a serious, ongoing two-way conversation between scientists and contemplatives.

Such dialogue has only become possible through recent advancements in technology paired with a mindset of genuine curiosity. While this book doesn't have any ambition to reflect these infinite connections between our various 'schools of thought', I hope that by allowing us to open many doors, rather than one or a few, it will enable the readers to find the door they want to go through. I hope it will lead them to the same living room.

As I continued experiencing being a father, husband and son, and supporting clients to help their organisations thrive, I found that my initial belief that I had nothing to add was irrelevant for another reason. Given that we have an abundance of information, knowledge, experience and wisdom available, if it was these things that transformed human behaviour and helped us be at our best as humans, then we would have peace and joy in our families, in our institutions and in ourselves. Clearly that is not yet the case and there's more work to be done. And that's OK. It's the reason we're here. It is not so much *knowing* that matters, but *seeing*.

With that in mind, I realised that I didn't necessarily need to be a lead singer to inspire my fellow humans. I can add my voice to a beautiful choir so that it can be heard and felt by more people. Although there's evidence to the contrary, I choose to believe that leadership must ultimately evolve in ways that allow our humanity to unfold fully rather than constraining it. Given we're living in managed societies, where organisations and how they're being led affect literally everyone's lives and even our planet, how else could we possibly tap into the abundant human energy, wisdom, creativity and perspective to deal with today's and tomorrow's challenges?

I've written this book for those to whom my voice can contribute and accompany them on their path. I've written this book for leaders who are on the doorstep.

Real fiction

This is not an academic book. Although grounded in research, it is a fictitious story – a conversation between our two protagonists, Maryam and Paul. Yet, while they don't actually exist, their questions and conversations do. You could call this book 'real fiction'.

In the tradition of many other wonderful books that use dialogue as a platform, I have used Paul and Maryam's encounters to reflect the themes that connect the countless conversations I have had over the past ten years or so, be they with clients, professional partners or loved ones. I have used either parts of conversations, or whole conversations that took place exactly as they are shared in this book. Whenever someone said, 'You know, I wondered...', I wanted to make the resultant conversation available to a broader audience.

I chose this path to make this a more *experiential* book. In the same way you might read a novel, attend a concert, or enjoy a sumptuous meal with your family, you will get the most from this book if you allow yourself to *experience* the conversations; if you choose to listen with your heart as much if not more than with your mind. There's certainly more to know than we can know about.

Puschendorf, June 2019

CHAPTER 1

Energy: The Foundation Of Performance

'I've learned that people will forget what you said,
people will forget what you did, but people will never
forget how you made them feel.'

Maya Angelou

'We actually respond to one another's energy
more than to people's exact words or actions.
In any situation, our taking or giving of energy is
what we are actually doing.'

Richard Rohr

For the first time, Maryam arrived to have lunch in the restaurant of the new firm she had joined only two months ago. Since she'd moved with her family into their new home and assumed the role of Senior Vice President of Emerging Markets, she had been travelling most of the time, meeting her team members, learning about the business from various colleagues, connecting with clients, and sitting in on important meetings with her project teams. While it had been quite a ride to this point, she had started to better understand the significant challenges her team would soon have to tackle.

She was happy with her new position and the significant step both she and her family had recently taken. She was grateful for the tremendous understanding and support of her husband, who'd quit his previous job to relocate, and her children who were mostly excited about their new school and the new group of friends they'd make.

The atmosphere in the restaurant intrigued Maryam. It felt like a busy marketplace on a Saturday morning in Italy – people were greeting one another, having conversations while waiting in line to order and pick up their food, and mingling at the tables and in the corridors. The place was buzzing with energy.

Maryam scanned the room and found an empty seat at a large table filled with a group of people busily engaged in conversation. She sat down, looked to her left and then to her right. She hadn't yet touched her food, enjoying the energy surrounding her. Unable to help but feel the need to pause and enjoy it, she was puzzled. Didn't she just want to grab a bite? Somehow, this place made her feel enlivened.

Deciding to make conversation with the people sitting next to her, she said, 'This is a great place, isn't it? It feels so special.'

People nodded back at her with smiles on their faces as if to say, 'Oh yes, very much so.'

She turned to her food and took a bite of her salmon steak. It was juicy and cooked perfectly. It tasted as if it could have come from an upscale restaurant in town.

'Wow, and the food is amazing!' she said spontaneously, surprising even herself.

'Thank you for the compliment,' a man sitting on the opposite side of the table said. 'I'll pass it on to the team.'

Maryam was again surprised. 'Oh, are you a member of the kitchen staff here?'

With a gentle smile, the man responded, 'Well, yes, you could say so.' He paused, extended his hand, and said, 'I'm Paul. Nice to meet you. I'm the chef and head of the restaurant.'

Maryam was puzzled.

Before she could reply, a loud voice yelled over the counter, 'Alright, everyone, listen up. We're not only here to provide you with calories. Although we do that really well, don't we?'

Someone yelled back light heartedly, 'I'm proof that you do!'

The employee behind the counter continued, 'So, if you want to find happiness, it's only one spoon away. Come over here and experience a taste of Moroccan cuisine. When you are done, you won't even have to travel there to get a feel for the country!'

Maryam turned around and saw a tall man in his forties, serving a few of his colleagues who had accepted his invitation. Laughing, he was saying, 'Hi, Sarah – good to see you again. Let me know how you like it, OK? I'm trying something new here.'

'Will do, Joe. Promise. See you soon.'

Paul spoke to Maryam. 'That's Joseph. He was on holiday in Morocco a few weeks ago, meeting with chefs and exploring some of the local cuisine. He loves doing that, and he is now trying out some of the recipes he discovered and fell in love with while he was there. He really enjoys trying new things, and frankly, he's competitive. I think he wants to come out on top of our monthly customer survey when people vote for "The dish I can't live without anymore".'

Maryam replied, 'I tell you what, Paul, I'm completely stunned by the energy here – it's everywhere. I mean it's in the room, in the people, and in the food. I've never experienced anything like that in a company restaurant... and I've seen and tasted' she smiled 'a lot of them. The food here is better than many of the fine-dining places I've visited recently. There's so much... not sure if I can say this... joy. There's joy here.'

Paul: 'Oh, thank you. It's made my day to hear you say that. We've come a long way, you know, and it wasn't always like that. When you share how you feel, I know we've done what we're actually here to do... what we are and what gives all us a buzz in the restaurant.'

Maryam: 'Oh... and what is that?'

Paul: 'Well, I feel I can't really put it in words. You see, using words is a bit like trying to tell someone about a wonderful piece of music. If one could convey the experience of it in words, then we wouldn't need the music, if you see what I mean? Essentially, what we seem to love here is... experiencing and being part of... *this*. When the team and I talk about what gives us a real buzz at work and in life... you know, the "spark of life", if you like... we all feel it's fundamentally about celebrating and nurturing the joy of life through great food and togetherness.'

Paul paused, looked around, then looked back at Maryam. 'You see, *that* unites us. It pulls us forward.'

'I see...' Maryam wasn't quite sure what to say. She was slightly bewildered by the directness and power of Paul's response to her outwardly bland question.

Maryam: 'You talk about the "spark of life" with your team? I would have guessed you'd spend most of your time planning and managing schedules, suppliers, costs and your staff.'

Paul: 'You're right. Of course, I do. We all do. But I've realised over time that my role as leader is first and foremost to nurture an energy that enables everyone to be their best, individually and as a team. I'm kind of the CEO of this division.'

Maryam: 'CEO?'

Paul: 'I'm the Chief Energy Officer. That's my role. All the rest follows from there.'

Maryam: 'Chief Energy Officer? I've never heard that term. Well, it is nice to meet you, Chief Energy Officer Paul. I haven't even introduced myself. I'm Maryam Johnston. I joined the company a few months ago as the new Head of Business Development for Emerging Markets.'

Paul: 'Pleased to meet you, Maryam. Welcome on board. I'm sure you'll love it.'

Maryam: 'Thank you. I've just come back from a visit to our regional branches. I got to know my team members and reviewed the different projects we are all working on. Lots of things to think about.'

She looked to her plate and took another bite of her salmon steak.

Maryam: 'Paul, I appreciate your openness. Yet, to be honest, I am a bit surprised by what you've just said. I thought that in your role, you'd deal with practical things. Forgive me if my question is a bit cheeky, but I assume your boss doesn't ask for an energy KPI at the end of the month, does he?'

Paul: 'Oh, that's not cheeky at all. Although I personally think it would be a good idea to have an energy KPI. Of course we look at budgets. I guess what I'm sharing with you is simply what I've realised for myself over the past few years here, especially during our journey of turning this restaurant around. You probably don't know this, but we had some rough years. This place was about to close.'

Maryam: 'Oh no, I had no idea. Well, you guys seem to have turned it around, haven't you?'

Paul: 'Yes. We are now looking back at some of the best years we've ever had. In fact, compared to other corporate restaurants, we are among the most profitable. More importantly, we score higher on all measures that affect our profits in the long run: customer satisfaction, health and safety, staff engagement and turnover, and cash flow.

'To get there, we did have to make significant changes and investments, including our supply chain, our equipment, our training and development, and even introducing a new IT system. It's been a challenging three-year journey, and we have just started conversations with the IT company at the front of our grounds to explore what it would take to accommodate 1,000 more people in this space. They want to close their restaurant down and use ours, which makes perfect sense since their people are often in here anyway. It doesn't make sense for them to run a restaurant on their own, so we might end up hiring some of their staff to accommodate this growth.'

Maryam: 'Wow, I had no idea how much you're growing. To be fair, I've only just moved here with my family, and it's the first time I've eaten here. Hmm... I guess I'd be happy if I could tell a similar success story three years from now. At the moment, it's not looking all that rosy for my division, I must say. There are tons of issues pressuring the team, like declining margins in most markets, and new competitors, and emerging technology trends we'll need to embrace. We're also discussing a new organisational structure, and some of my team members don't seem to be in a good place. One very experienced team member left a month after my arrival to join one of our competitors. There's something about this place that seems to make it harder to get things done. I can't quite put my finger on it.'

Paul: 'I can relate to that. As I mentioned, when I first arrived we needed to make some substantial changes as well. Some of them were pretty straightforward, others more complex. But the most important one that enabled and then accelerated all these practical changes was a shift in our energy, or a *shift of hearts*, as I sometimes call it.'

Maryam raised her eyebrows, expressing her surprise, and then responded after a brief pause.

'Well, I can certainly feel a great positive energy here. But why do you feel it is so pivotal to your performance and to the success of what you've been doing?'

Paul: 'Oh, thank you, Maryam, for asking that. I am not asked about this very often, so I'm grateful for your curiosity. You see, more and more I've come to realise that energy is at the heart of leadership. And while some things have become much clearer to me, I'm still discovering.'

Paul glanced at the large clock at the far end of the room. 'Given that we will both need to return to our work soon, maybe I could offer a few views on your question while we are having our coffees, and we could talk more another time, if you would see value in that. I often feel that new perspectives come through dialogue with curious people like you.'

Maryam: 'Oh, Paul, that would be wonderful. Let me grab a coffee for both of us. Espresso?'

Paul: 'Ah, yes. Single espresso, please.'

Maryam went to the café bar that was only a few steps away from their table and returned moments later with two cups of espresso.

Paul: 'Thank you, Maryam. Well, to explore your question a bit around why energy seems so pivotal to me, can I ask you a question?'

Maryam: 'Sure. Go ahead.'

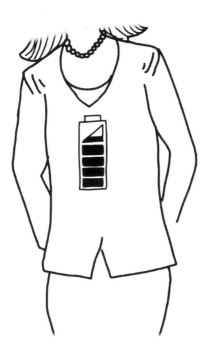

Paul: 'Imagine for a moment people in your team had 10% more positive energy than they bring to work every day right now. Imagine they'd bring 10% more ideas to meetings and conversations every day. Then people would speak their mind during meetings 10% more often because they'd feel safe enough to do so, and they'd listen with curiosity to what they hear. People would actively find out in 10% more instances how else they could support or interact with customers in ways that would make them rave about our organisation. What would that do for the performance of your department and the challenges in front of you?'

Maryam, laughing: 'Well, I guess, at a minimum, it would be equivalent to increasing my staff by 40% or more... for free. And it would address many of the things that seem to be slowing us down at the moment.'

Paul: 'Now, imagine on top of that, you could spend 10% less of your own energy and time resolving differences among team members or divisions because they would resolve them on their own and in a healthy way.'

Maryam: 'I'm not sure how to calculate that, but I guess all of that combined would improve my performance, and that of my team, by at least 50%.'

Paul: 'And why would that be the case in your experience?'

Maryam: 'Well, because it would improve the speed and quality of what we do, and help us meet our goals with less wear and tear. We would have more and even better ideas. We would probably agree on what needs to get done and by whom more quickly, possibly without my constant involvement. I believe people would be more engaged and committed to execute plans, and also adjust more quickly when we hit speed bumps along the way.'

Paul: 'That makes sense to me. Now, imagine if on top of that, when people in your team are asked by family members and friends how they feel about their work, 10% more often they say "Grateful", "Valued" or even "Inspired"... words of that nature... What would that do for you?'

Maryam didn't say anything. She just thought, *We'd have less turnover and I would enjoy my work more too.*

Paul: 'Now, in my experience, these attitudes and behaviours are not so much a result of compensation plans, trainings or processes, although all of them matter; first of all, they are a result of how people *feel* – which simply reflects the *human energy* in our organisation.'

Maryam: 'It's a really nice idea, Paul, but where do you *find* this energy? It doesn't exactly grow on trees. I'm not here to energise people, especially since they're all grown-ups, and mostly well-paid ones, too. And I'm not the kind of leader who gives inspiring talks or builds camaraderie by telling funny jokes all the time. In the end, it's business, not football. And I don't think we're going to have a motivational speaker every month or spend even more money on our leadership development budget.'

Paul: 'Maryam – there's no need to. The energy you need is already here. You just haven't been able to fully tap into it at the moment.'

Maryam: 'What makes you say that? I mean, you haven't met my team yet, but I can assure you that I don't see the kind of energy levels you're talking about in them. That is going to take some work on my part.'

Paul: 'Oh, I'm sure you will do something. The way I see it is that our energy isn't so much a *finite* resource that needs to be replenished, a bit like putting fuel in a car or a battery. It is more like an *infinite* resource that can be *blocked* from self-replenishing and being accessed. So, when energy, or the quality of energy is low, the question to ask is less how to *inject* more energy from the outside. That would be a bit like trying to fill an ocean with more water through a hose. The real question is, how do you get rid of the obstacles that *block* the access to the sources of energy which are always there? In other words, can you tap into the ocean?'

Maryam: 'Well, that's a great question. Easier said than done, I suppose. So, how would I do that?'

Paul: 'Oh, I don't have a recipe for that.'

Maryam smiled. 'Based on the energy I'm sensing here and your success, I think you do. I mean, this place is really "cooking".'

Paul laughed. 'Well, in a sense, we are all chefs, aren't we? For you to *enjoy* being a cook and inspire others with your own unique cuisine, I recommend adapting and developing the approaches that you feel work for you and your team. What I can offer you are some of the *ingredients* that I use when I'm cooking. These ingredients are both *simple* and *universal*. They are also always *available*, no matter where, when, or how you cook. They are used in many of the recipes and cookery books you'll come across. Some have been around for thousands of years, and some have been better researched and understood in recent years. You see, I'm just rediscovering their great value and integrating them into what I'm doing. And over time, I've learned how to become a better cook using these same simple, universal ingredients.'

Maryam: 'That sounds great. So, what are these ingredients?'

Paul: 'Well, I can't describe them. They are not so much things or tools, rather sources or channels that help you to better tap into the ocean. They are not really separate, as they work together, as any recipe would. Yet if we want to break them down for a moment, then I'd call them mind, heart, spirit and body.'

Paul paused for a moment.

Paul: Maybe it's better to call them areas of awareness. You see, you can only shift things you are aware of, right?'

Maryam: 'Hmm, indeed.'

Paul: 'Paying attention to these areas has helped me to become more mindful – more aware, if you like – of those things that help nurture performance by accessing energy and transforming lower forms of energy into higher ones when needed.'

Maryam: 'Paul, I would certainly be interested to hear more about these areas of awareness. I'm wondering, though, why you focus so much on energy in the first place. I mean, the things you've talked about – and that we'd all like to have, I guess, like supporting each other more – seem to be common sense, right? For example, shouldn't people simply know how to get things done in a supportive way? Don't you think that when someone is not collaborating that it basically comes down to a lack of experience or training – or maybe a lack of character or respect? Why don't you just tell people what to do and set better expectations?'

Paul: 'I sense a bit of frustration in your words, and that's OK. I used to think and feel exactly like you do, even asking myself the same questions. And of course, there is great value in setting clear expectations. However, I didn't quite get the results I'd hoped for, even when I set crystal-clear goals, so I asked myself, "If people's actions were predominantly based on intellect, information, and knowledge or skill, then why would I face any challenges in nurturing the attitudes and behaviours I wanted to achieve?" I could just give everyone a book, right?'

Maryam: 'Yes, that makes sense.'

Paul: 'Maryam – let me ask you this. Think about having to choose between four different types of bananas in a supermarket. Two have a bio-label and two don't. They have four different prices and weights, come from different countries, and all look slightly different. Would you develop a decision-making algorithm to help you?'

Maryam: 'I could, but it would take too much time.'

Paul: 'So how would you decide?'

Maryam: 'Hmm. With my gut, I guess.'

Paul: 'So, you'd *sense* the right decision. You'd *feel* it.'

Maryam: 'Yeah, I guess you could say that.'

Paul: 'In my experience, mere information or knowledge alone doesn't change, let alone transform, human behaviour. For example, there's ample research on the impact of sugar or smoking on our health. There are hundreds of documentaries, books and information campaigns to promote awareness on these topics. If information alone shifted our behaviour, then no one would be smoking or over-indulging on sugary products, right?'

Maryam: 'Hmmm...'

Paul: 'It seems to me that we decide much more with our hearts than with our minds. When it comes to daily behaviour or actions, our intellect plays the role of a government spokesperson. It receives the information last and then needs to justify all decisions.'

Maryam: 'In other words, we make the decision before it even reaches our conscious mind.'

Paul: 'Yes, you could say that. For example, you described your experience here as something that felt great.'

Maryam: 'Yes, that's right, I did. I just love the energy.'

Paul: 'So, is it fair to say that you can actually *feel* energy?'

Maryam: 'Yeah, I do pick up a vibration.'

Paul: 'Now, would you say that your own energy changes over the course of a day? I mean, do you feel different as the day progresses?'

Maryam: 'Yes, of course. Many times during the day.'

Paul: 'And would you agree that you're *always* feeling something. In other words, you cannot *not* feel?'

Maryam: 'Sure.'

Paul: 'And are there moments when you experience more – let's say – *positive* energy, and other times when you feel more *negative* energy?'

Maryam: 'Oh yes, I do. How did you know?'

Paul: 'Well, because chances are, you are human too.'

Maryam and Paul smiled at one another.

Paul: 'OK, now put that aside for a moment, and let me ask you this. What are some of the behaviours, attitudes or guiding principles that made you successful in your personal life and in your professional life as a leader? I mean, what kind of advice would you give to young leaders if they asked you how to become more successful?'

Maryam, smiling: 'People ask me that question all of the time in almost every leadership seminar I attend. But I'm not always sure I can answer it.'

Paul: 'Well, just share a few of your thoughts. Tell me what comes to mind first.'

Maryam: 'Let me see. For a start, I think it's been my ability to listen to people, and then... my capacity to collaborate with others. What else... I have developed an ability to adjust to other people and be more flexible. You know, things never turn out the way you've planned them in your mind.'

Paul: 'OK, great. Anything else?'

Maryam: 'I've also realised I am pretty resilient in the face of obstacles or setbacks. After a while, I tend to overcome these challenges and end up somehow stronger and more mature.'

Paul: 'Thank you. That makes all the sense in the world. I can see how these traits got you here, and I guess there is a lot more to it. I wish at times I were a little more resilient and flexible, like you.'

Paul paused for a moment. 'Are there ever moments when you *don't* display these qualities or when they seem less *accessible* to you? I mean, are there any moments when you aren't that great a listener? Or maybe times when you aren't as flexible as you could be?'

Maryam: 'Of course. That can happen.'

Paul: 'Well, you are not alone. And, are there other moments when you feel like these qualities are simply part of you, and you demonstrate them quite naturally and effortlessly, even in a difficult situation?'

Maryam reflected for a moment.

Maryam: 'Most of the time, I'm not really thinking about my strengths. I'm thinking about handling the situation in front of me. But yes, there are moments when I feel like I'm in the zone.'

Paul: 'I would suggest that in those moments when your strengths aren't as available to you, it is not as if you've forgotten them. They didn't go away, you just had less access to them.'

Maryam: 'It is like there is a knot in the hose that connects me with the ocean.'

Paul: 'Indeed. Now think back to the different energy states you've just mentioned. You said that sometimes they are higher, and other times they are lower, right?'

Maryam: 'That's right.'

Paul: 'When would you say that you have more access to those strengths of yours? Is it when you experience a higher level of energy or a lower one?'

Maryam: 'Oh, I see your point. There is a correlation.'

Paul: 'Yes, I believe there is.'

Maryam took a sip of her coffee, reflecting on her conversation with Paul. 'That's interesting. If I'm always feeling something, then my energy would affect literally *every* thought, *every* conversation, *every* decision, and *every* action throughout my day, right? It would define what we call *performance*, which is merely the result of this.'

Paul: 'That's my understanding. Now if you see yourself as the Chief Energy Officer in your organisation, then your guiding question becomes how can you *awaken* positive energy across your team, *transform* negative energy, and then *direct* that energy towards a shared purpose? Energy becomes your main asset, simply because it affects *everything*.'

Maryam: 'I hadn't looked at it this way. Thank you, Paul. I really want to continue exploring these thoughts, but I think it's time we both returned to work.'

Paul: 'Yes, I should go back, too. Maryam, having this conversation with you, and of course hearing how much you enjoyed our place has given *me* a lot more energy for the rest of my day.'

Maryam: 'I would love to hear more about the principles and how they have helped you to actually transform energy... or make a shift of hearts, as you called it. Would you mind if we continued our conversation another time?'

Paul: 'It would be my pleasure. Why don't you come to one of our team meetings next week? We have a team huddle at 6.30am each day, an hour before the restaurant opens for breakfast. And we could have breakfast here together after the meeting.'

Maryam: 'That sounds great... how about Wednesday?'

Paul: 'Wednesday it is.'

Maryam: 'It was a blessing to meet you today. I'm looking forward to seeing you again.'

Journaling

Maryam arrived at her office. She sat quietly behind her desk and gazed out of the window. Something was happening for her, as if something inside, that had been stuck, had now started moving again. After a moment of sitting there silently, a thought crossed her mind. She opened a drawer in her desk and took out a beautiful empty notebook. It was a gift from her husband, George, who found it in a small store during his travels in India. She loved the texture of it, its weight when holding it in her hands, the colours of the cover and pages, even the smell. When he gave it to her he said, 'I know you're on a journey. Maybe this can be your logbook. A space for contemplation.' He'd left a note on the first page: 'Write as if no one is reading. Love, George.' Since then the journal had been patiently sitting there, waiting for its moment to come. Today Maryam knew what it was for. She opened a page and started jotting down thoughts and questions that emerged from her encounter with Paul...

- Human performance is a function of human energy, a function of how we *feel*.

- Our strengths show up more often in positive energy states, and are less accessible when we are in less positive energy states.

- Human energy is not a finite source, like fuel. It is an infinite source that is always available, yet not always accessible. It can be blocked.

- My role is less to inject energy, than to awaken it or remove the obstacles.

- What would happen if people in my organisation and myself had access to and felt our positive energy just 10% more often?

- What would I do differently, what questions would I ask, what would I pay attention to, if I considered energy to be our main asset... if I was the Chief Energy Officer?

- The Chief Energy Officer guiding question: How else could I nurture positive energy, transform negative energy, and then direct the human energy towards a shared purpose?

CHAPTER 2

Feelings: Our State Of Heart

'The most crucial use of knowledge and education is to understand the importance of developing a good heart.'

Dalai Lama

'God will break your heart over and over and over and over again until it stays open.'

Rumi

It was Wednesday morning. Maryam was just entering the parking deck. She had been reflecting on her encounter with Paul. His idea of energy sounded interesting – it made sense to her, and seemed relevant to what she faced every day. But then she wasn't sure how to translate his idea into action. It was all a bit too abstract, almost idealistic and naïve. At the same time, she couldn't ignore what she had experienced in the restaurant, and the stories she kept on hearing about how successful Paul's approach had become. Paul seemed to be a seasoned businessman, too. She felt puzzled, interested and sceptical.

'I need to understand this better,' she told herself. 'I want to know what being a Chief Energy Officer truly means for Paul.'

When she got into her car, she realised that she was running late. She rushed into the restaurant, seeing Paul and the team in the middle of their daily huddle. Not wanting to disturb them, she slowly approached the team, trying to make eye contact with Paul. Once he saw her, she made a gesture to signal that she would wait until they'd finished.

Paul: 'Hi, Maryam, please come and join us. We're almost finished.'

Maryam came closer. 'Thanks. Good morning, everyone.'

The team responded with warm welcomes. Joseph, the chef who had been preparing the Moroccan cuisine last week, said, 'Good to have you here, we haven't seen you for a few days.'

Paul redirected the conversation. 'OK, Sue, you were talking about the frustration you experienced with the new cashier system. Please carry on. How are you feeling, and what is causing that for you?'

Maryam listened to the conversation. She noted the sense of curiosity and inquiry coming from both Paul and other team members following Sue's observations. Some just asked, 'What else did you notice?' helping her to express what was on her mind and understand the situation more fully. Others asked, 'What might we have missed?' and 'What do we need to understand better here?' and 'What could we do to deal with this today until we find a solution?'

Maryam also noted their unusually appreciative tone. Sometimes it was expressed in a gesture as someone was talking about an idea or asking a question. Sometimes people simply said, 'Ah, that's a great question. Thanks for bringing that up, hadn't thought about that.' They agreed on a workaround for the day, and to have a separate meeting involving only three of them after lunch to understand more deeply what they could learn from the situation. Some team members added, 'We're here if you need anything, OK?'

At the end of the meeting, Maryam and Paul went to the coffee bar at the back of the restaurant. People were starting to pass by to grab a coffee or drink on their way to the office or to chat with colleagues at the bar, but most of the tables were free this time of the day. Maryam and Paul sat in a corner where they could oversee the little plaza in front of the main entrance.

Maryam: 'You seem to pay a lot of attention to the tone in your meetings.'

Paul: 'That's true. As CEO...'

Maryam: 'Chief Energy Officer...'

Paul: 'Yes... noticing how people feel, which is both reflected in and influenced by their tone, really matters a lot to me.'

Maryam: 'You want to create a nice atmosphere, right?'

Paul: 'Well, that's helpful, but it's about more than that. In the end, I can only change what I'm aware of. And I can only be aware of what I pay attention to. If you want to change the cash flow or customer satisfaction of your business, you'd pay attention to it, right?'

Maryam: 'For sure.'

Paul: 'Well, tone is no different. It reflects the energy of your team.'

Maryam: 'OK, sure. But how would it actually help me to know how my team feels? In the end, we need to get a job done, no matter how we feel. I mean, we're all grown-ups here, and I can't always talk with people about how they feel before they do something. Don't you agree?'

Paul thought for a moment. Then he asked Maryam if she had a piece of paper and a pen with her. She took out the notebook in which she had started writing her reflections from their previous conversation.

Paul: 'Can you think of moments when you feel like your best self... you know, things come easily?'

Maryam: 'Yes, that happens. And what would you like me to do?'

Paul: 'Bring to mind these moments and write down any words that would describe how you feel then.'

Maryam took a few moments, wrote down a few words, and then shared her list with Paul.

- at peace
- happy
- grateful
- joyful
- enthusiastic
- light hearted
- energised
- curious
- alert

Paul: 'OK, it sounds like you are in a good place. Now, can I ask you to make another list below reflecting how you tend to deal with the world then? I mean, how do you react to situations and people around you when you feel that way? How do you get things done? What do you do, or not do?'

Maryam gave some thought to Paul's question and created another list of words. After a short while, she turned her notebook around and shared it with Paul.

- at peace
- happy
- grateful
- joyful
- enthusiastic
- light hearted
- energised
- curious
- alert
- resilient
- getting on with things
- ideas and clarity come to me more easily
- connecting with people
- supportive of others and asking for help
- sense of humour
- seeing best in others
- focussed
- calm, keeping perspective under stress
- listening, more open to others views

Maryam: 'Hmmm...I guess I tend to deal with things with more perspective. I often have a sense of humour in dealing with challenges that pop up. I don't mean I'm cynical; I'm light hearted, yet focused and determined. I often involve others quite easily. And when things go wrong, I tend to be more forgiving, both with others and with myself. I'm enjoying work... and life more broadly.'

Paul: 'It sounds like you're at your best then. Is there anything else you notice?'

Maryam: 'Yes... I generally tend to make much better decisions. Sometimes I don't know why. I guess I trust my gut.'

Paul: 'Yes, that's true for me too.'

Maryam: 'So, I'm effective when I feel good, right? But I'm not quite sure why you're asking. I mean, I know that.'

Paul: 'Well, do you ever have a not-so-good moment or day?'

Maryam: 'Yes, of course... welcome to my life. I guess in roles like mine, people have to deal with the not-so-good things, right?'

Paul: 'Maybe... Would you mind repeating what you just did and reflect on how you feel in these moments or days?'

Maryam laughed. 'OK, that's easy.' She turned the page and wrote down her thoughts.

Maryam: 'OK, here's what I'm aware of. I tend to feel kind of nervous on a not-so-good day. I'm tense; my chest is tense. If I'm completely honest, I'm worried. For example, I may be feeling concerned about how a client might react to a proposal, or how my boss will react. I also feel overwhelmed at times, like I can't cope with what's happening or likely to happen around me. The truth is I feel insecure. But don't tell anyone, OK?'

Paul: 'Well, you're not alone in that, I guess. Thank you for sharing this with me. I feel grateful for your openness and candour.'

They smiled at each other. Somehow, they both enjoyed a sense of connectedness and safety in each other's presence.

Paul: 'Now when you feel that way, what's different about how you show up and deal with things?'

Maryam: 'Please promise you won't tell anyone. Although some will know anyway. I can get quite upset. My voice changes and I react... I sometimes interrupt what I'm doing to respond to an email. I engage in arguments more easily, and at times I tend to exaggerate a bit to win the argument, and I will... Do you want me to carry on?'

Paul: 'Maryam, thank you so much for sharing that so openly with me. Would you mind writing it below the feelings you've already jotted down?'

- worried
- concerned
- tense
- irritated, upset
- overwhelmed
- insecure
- feel misunderstood
- angry
- guilty

- more aggressive in tone (also emails)
- defensive
- self-righteous
- quick to judge & argue
- harder to focus
- little/no clarity, thinking feels hard
- little energy, less courage

Maryam: 'So then why are you asking this? I have bad moments at times. We all do, don't we?'

Paul: 'Indeed, we do. It's simply part of being human. Now, if you look at it, you seem to be describing two different Maryam's, right?'

Maryam: 'Yeah, you're right.'

Paul: But it's the same you – the same eyes, ears, and brain, the same arms and legs. Yet depending on how you feel, you seem to literally see the world differently. And you then act differently, too.'

Maryam: 'Yes, I can see that.'

Paul: 'Now, consider that the world around you – the people, the emails, the meetings, and the situations – are actually the same. They haven't changed, but you have. More precisely, your state of heart has shifted – and with it, that which you are able to see in the very same situations and people.'

Maryam: 'That's interesting. I hadn't looked at it that way. But what exactly do you mean by "state of heart"?'

Paul: 'Well, you can experience hundreds of different feelings, and there are probably even more ways of describing them. But fundamentally, it seems to me there are only two main groups of feelings. I call them "states of heart", because your heart can be either open or closed. You see, feelings like worry, anxiety, insecurity, irritation, bother, anger, or resentment are just different words for or degrees of fear. It's either the fear of losing something you have or are attached

'If you can choose to listen to your feelings even more, and notice the state of heart you're in, then you can literally use it as a guide.'

35

to, the fear of not getting something you desire, or the fear of an experience you would like to avoid. I call these feelings connected with fear "closed states of heart".

'Now, when you feel inspired, grateful, excited, light hearted, confident, curious, optimistic, understanding, compassionate, forgiving, peaceful or joyful, you are in an "open state of heart". All these feelings are essentially different manifestations of love towards others, yourself and life.'

Maryam added 'open state of heart' at the top of her first list and 'closed state of heart' above the second list.

Paul: 'Now, have a look at your lists. If you can choose to listen to your feelings even more, and notice the state of heart you're in, then you can literally use it as a guide. Your state of heart reflects how effective you are at any given moment in time.'

Maryam: 'Oh, so it's a bit like a dashboard in a car, but rather than showing my speed and the health of my engine, it reflects my effectiveness?'

Paul: 'I love that analogy. Yes, it's like a dial showing you the temperature of your engine. When it's too hot, you'd probably stop your car to see what's up, or at least drive a bit slower so you don't break down. You are aware that you can't fully rely on your engine in this moment. When the dial indicates a normal temperature, you can basically trust the engine is working fine and don't give it any more thought. But imagine for a moment you didn't have that information in your car...'

Maryam, jokingly: 'Well, I guess I'd need to buy a new car more often.'

Paul: 'Probably. Now, as a human being, you have a built-in indicator. Isn't that great? Your state of heart tells you how things are going for you at any given moment. Once you start noticing it, you can treat it as a valuable piece of information, rather than something to suppress or ignore. Equipped with that information, you can make better choices at work or at home.'

Maryam: 'Hmm, I've never looked at my feelings as information. Rather I've always felt they are something to be managed and removed from business. I often say, "Let's keep emotions out of this" or "Don't be so emotional".'

Paul: 'My guess is you wouldn't ignore a piece of information about the state of the company, or the state of a major project, would you?'

Maryam: 'Of course not. I'd probably pay a lot of attention to it.'

Paul: 'However, when it comes to our state as humans, I'm not so sure we do that all the time. Instead, we can ignore our state of heart, and that of others, and just carry on driving.'

Maryam: 'At times, when the indicators are red, we might even put things in high gear.'

Her words put a smile on Paul's face. They both giggled.

Paul: 'Now, on the other hand, when we are in an open state of heart – simply put – we tend to be more effective, more creative, more collaborative, and more resilient when faced with setbacks or challenges than when we are in a more closed state of heart.'

Maryam: 'There is more energy available to us – I mean, to the car. The pipes connecting me with the ocean are open.'

Paul: 'I love our car analogy even more now.'

Maryam opened a new page in her notebook and drew a picture.

Paul: 'Maryam, I would want to pause and consider what you've just mentioned about the pipes which connect us with the ocean. You see, in my view, we always have the capacity to be collaborative, creative, resilient and focused... all those qualities that we need to be productive. We are *born* this way, some of us might be born with or have developed bigger pipes throughout our lives. You and I will need to recruit our teams accordingly. However, most of the time, when the people we work display these capacities less than needed, it is not as if they lack skill, experience, information or knowledge. It's their *access* to their innate resources that is limited. Our job is to help them open up their pipes.'

Maryam: 'To shift their state of heart...'

Paul: 'Yes.'

Maryam: 'Carry on, Paul. Tell me a little more about this.'

Paul: 'Let me see. You've mentioned that you have said or done things that you later regretted when you were in a closed state of heart, right?'

Maryam: 'Yes.'

Paul: 'So, what might you have done differently if you had simply noticed and accepted that you were in a closed state of heart?'

Maryam paused. 'Well, I might have chosen to simply not react immediately in order not to cause any unnecessary damage.'

Paul: 'Why not?'

Maryam: 'Because when I'm in a closed state of heart, I'm not really thinking straight. In a sense, my brain jumps out of the window.'

Paul laughed. 'Oh, that's such a lovely way of putting it. I need to share that with my team. So, if you look at how you've experienced yourself in differed states of heart, how would you describe how you tend to look at things when you are in a more open state of heart?'

Maryam: 'Well, I would simply say, with a greater sense of perspective.'

Paul: 'I feel the same way. When I'm in a closed state of heart, it's like looking at things in Google Maps street view. I can see what's in front of, next to and behind me. But when I look at things from an open state of heart, I can look at people and situations from a helicopter's perspective. I can see further and become more aware of connections occurring all around me. And I might realise how things look from the perspective of another person and why he or she actually has a hard time seeing what I'm seeing... and vice versa.'

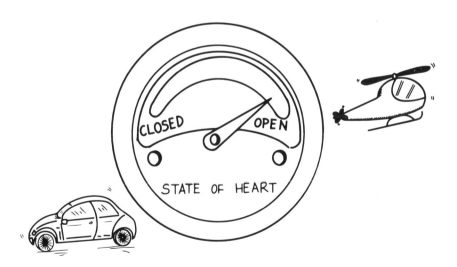

Maryam: 'So, in a sense, our company is a network of constantly opening and closing hearts, with people shifting from street view to helicopter view.'

Paul: 'I think so.'

Maryam felt a need to pause and reflect. She looked out of the window, observing the people who were walking into the office building, imagining open and closed hearts in each of them as they went to work in front of their PCs, on the phone or in a meeting with colleagues, customers or business partners.

With awareness comes choice

Maryam: 'I'm seeing more clearly the relation between my state of heart and the outcomes in my personal and professional life. But is it really that simple? I mean, in my world there's enough stuff happing, even during one day, that might lead to a permanent shut down of my heart. I still need to get results, regardless of my state of heart. And I do.'

Paul: 'Well, yes, it is simple. Or, as an old friend of mine put it, it's simple but not simplistic. And yes, indeed, my heart opens and closes all the time.'

Maryam: 'I'm relieved. So, what do you do about it?'

Paul: 'Well, unfortunately, I have no recipe for that either. To begin with, I'd say there's nothing right or wrong about having an open or closed state of heart. It's all part of being human, I guess. For example, have you ever been angry?'

Maryam: 'Yes, course.'

Paul: 'No worries. Welcome to the human race. I guess there's an angry three-year-old in all of us, secretly wishing a tantrum would help us get what we want, right?'

Maryam: 'At times, mine occupies a whole bedroom in my mind.'

Paul: 'Now, I think there's a difference between *being* angry and being *aware* we're angry – because with awareness comes choice.'

Maryam: 'Like the choice not to say what I'm about to say because my brain has jumped out of the window?'

'With awareness comes choice, because I can only shift what I'm aware of.'

Paul, giggling: 'For example, your state of heart tells you the engine temperature. Now, there are certainly things you could do to cool the temperature down, or to ensure the motor runs more smoothly in the future. When you notice it's overheated, you will probably start with pulling the car over. However, if you don't look at the dashboard, *having* the indicator won't help you. To become aware, you have to first look.'

Maryam: 'I can see that.'

Paul: 'When you notice early enough that your state of heart is closing, because you've practised being a bit more mindful of your dashboard, one thing you might choose to do is tell yourself to keep your heart open, just for a bit longer.'

Maryam: 'And that works?'

Paul: 'Don't take my word for it. Try it.'

Maryam: 'So you're saying there's value in knowing how I feel in both open and closed states of heart, right?'

Paul: 'Yes, absolutely. You see, the heat-sensors that are displayed in the dashboard *notice* the motor temperature. They don't *judge* it for being too hot or too cold.'

They both paused a moment, and Maryam made a note: 'My state of heart is a dashboard, not a judge'.

Paul: 'And, of course, sometimes, even if you notice, you will go ahead and do what you feel like doing anyway, simply because you *can*. That is when your autopilot takes over.'

Maryam: 'That's exactly how I feel sometimes. Seems like you know me.'

Paul: 'Even then, being aware that
it's your closed state of heart causing
you to see things the way you are
seeing them and react the way you are
reacting, rather than the other person,
can help you to approach that person again
more easily. It might feel easier to reconcile. And,
if you choose to reflect on what happened, you get to know your
autopilot better. You can't fail; you only become more aware.'

'My state of
heart is a dashboard,
not a judge.'

Maryam: 'Paul, I'm noticing that you don't seem to attach a judgment to the different states of heart, right?'

Paul: 'Yes, that's right. You see, while life and work are probably
more fulfilling when you are in an open state of heart, there is
value in purely being aware of any state of heart, and accepting it
without judgment – almost with tenderness...'

Maryam: '... because with awareness comes choice.'

Paul: 'Indeed. And there's more to it than that. Imagine you are
angry, and then you get upset with yourself about the fact that you
are angry. Have you ever done that?'

Maryam: 'Oh, yeah.'

Paul: 'What does that do to your state of heart?'

Maryam: 'It closes even more. And then I get even more upset
while trying to suppress my emotions.'

Paul: 'Now, imagine you simply tell yourself, "I'm angry. I see it. I
fully accept it".'

> 'The pain we're experiencing often doesn't come so much from the emotion itself, but from us judging and not accepting it.'

Maryam: 'Well, ironically, I think the emotion would loosen its grip on me a bit.'

Paul: 'The pain we're experiencing often doesn't come so much from the emotion itself, but from us judging and not accepting it. Because we are all of our experiences, judging or rejecting negative emotions is like fighting reality and rejecting a part of ourselves. It's like cutting off a piece of our body.'

Maryam, with a gentle grin: 'Well, that hurts.'

Paul, laughing: 'Doesn't it?'

The Chief Energy Officer's role

Maryam: 'I'm thinking back over the role of the Chief Energy Officer. To be frank, at first it sounded a bit over the top, but now I'm thinking that if the quality of every thought, every conversation, every decision, every relationship – fundamentally the bloodstream of any organisation – is in essence a result of our state of heart, then paying attention to the state of heart of our company really is a central leadership capability. And, ironically, it seems to me we're making some of our most important decisions – those that actually require the most perspective – when our states of heart are rather closed.'

Paul: 'Yes, I think so too. For a Chief Energy Officer, the role of leadership comes down to four guiding questions: "What else can I do to spend more time in open states of heart, and help others to do the same?", "How can I help myself and others to limit the damage when we are in more closed states of heart?", "How can I transform closed states of heart into more open ones?" and "What do I want my organisation to focus its human energy on, and why?"'

Maryam: 'Hmm, I haven't looked at leadership, including my own role, this way before. Of course, I care about how people are doing, and I pay attention to it. But it didn't guide my daily choices.'

Paul: 'Well, that's great. You are sensing how people feel. Moving forward, you might simply want to pause more often and ask yourself, "How do I want people to feel as a result of this conversation with me, or this email I'm about to send?" or "If I said this, will the recipient feel stronger or weaker?" or "What will the impact be on their dashboard?"'

Maryam: 'Hmmm... that makes all the sense in the world to me now, but I would still like to talk more about how I can shift my states of heart and help others do the same. However, I don't want to take up too much of your time – I guess the restaurant doors will be opening in a few minutes, right?'

Paul, checking his watch: 'Indeed. Your question is a great starting point for when we meet next time. I enjoy our conversations, and I get so many ideas from talking with you. I'm still smiling about the brain jumping out of the window.'

Maryam: 'Thank you, Paul. Well, I'm in a helicopter state now, and I guess that will help me today. When can we meet next?'

Paul: 'If the weather is good, we could have a walk in the park next to us. Shall we say Friday afternoon, after five? Things quieten down here then.'

Maryam: 'That works for me. Friday it is.'

They left each other after a quick hug, both feeling profound gratitude for the mutual care and curiosity they'd experienced.

Journaling

It turned out to be a long and intense day, and it was only later in the evening that Maryam found some quiet time to herself to reflect back on their conversation. She sat on the couch, on her favourite spot, with a cup of her preferred tea that filled the air around her with a peaceful smell. Maryam loved sitting here – it gave her a sense of comfort and warmth. It was the place where she most enjoyed reading and reflecting, or just winding down.

Maryam picked up her journal, and glanced at her notes and her state of heart doodle. For a while she looked out of the old window in front of her. Then, as thoughts occurred, she added them to her journal…

- At any time, my state of heart is in one of two fundamental states

  » Open: when I experience feelings connected with love

  » Closed: when I experience feelings connected with fear

- My state of heart changes constantly.

- The world looks differently to me, depending on the state of heart I'm in.

- In more open states of heart, I tend to have more perspective, think more clearly and creatively, and act more wisely than in more closed states of heart – regardless of the situation I'm facing.

- In more closed states of heart, our brains tend to jump out of the window. I can hence use my state of heart as a dashboard.

- This dashboard tells me little about what's happening around me. Rather it is letting me know my own moment-to-moment capacity to deal with what is happening in my life.

- I can only shift what I'm aware of, including my state of heart. With awareness comes choice... and power.

- The emotional pain we're experiencing often comes not from the unpleasant emotion itself, but from us judging and rejecting it.

Four Chief Energy Officer questions:

1. What can I do to spend more time in open states of heart, and help others to do the same?

2. How can I help myself and others to limit the damage, when we are in more closed states of heart?

3. How can I transform closed states of heart into more open ones?

4. What do I want my organisation to focus its human energy on, and why?

CHAPTER 3

Thoughts: The Bridge To Our Heart

'It's not what you look at that matters,
it's what you see.'

Henry David Thoreau

'The only true action takes place in thought.'

Laura Basha

Maryam was running late the following Friday. Some of her meetings had lasted longer than she'd hoped. After a slightly late and rushed lunch, she texted Paul and suggested they meet in her office rather than at the park, hoping this would save some time.

Paul arrived at her office door just as she finished sending her last email of the day.

Maryam: 'Hi, Paul. Good to see you! Thank you so much for coming over and meeting me here. It's been a bit chaotic today.'

Paul: 'Hello, Maryam. No worries at all. I enjoyed the short walk and I am excited to see your office as well. I like it a lot.'

Maryam invited Paul to sit with her at a small table with two chairs in front of her desk.

Maryam: 'Coffee? Espresso? Tea? Or would you like some water?'

Paul: 'Oh yes, an espresso would be great. Thanks.'

Maryam prepared two cups of espresso from a machine that her husband and children had given her as a birthday gift. She kept the birthday card in a small wooden frame next to the coffee machine. Paul spotted it and read out the words.

'"Mum, when you wake up early, when you go to bed late, we know it's your love for us driving you. We love you, too." Is this a gift from your family?'

Maryam smiled and nodded.

Paul: 'What a lovely thought.'

Maryam: 'Yes. The coffee warms my body, and the thought warms my heart.'

Paul: 'I can imagine that.'

After putting cups of espresso for Paul and herself on the table, Maryam sat opposite him.

Paul: 'So, Maryam, how have you been since we last met?'

Maryam: 'Oh, it's been busy, and my team and I have accomplished quite a lot. And, I... I'm intrigued by the impact our conversation about the state of heart has had on me and my colleagues this week.'

Paul: 'I would love to hear about your experience.'

Maryam: 'I drew a little state of heart dashboard on the first page of my notebook. Here, have a look.'

Maryam: 'I look at it during a call or a conversation, quietly asking myself, "Where am I right now?" And you know, I've started noticing my state of heart.'

Paul: 'Oh, that's wonderful. And what did that do for you? What did you notice?'

Maryam: 'Well, for example, this Tuesday, I sat in a meeting where one of the regional directors shared an update on a major project we're working on together, He started sharing his frustration in front of everyone about working with the headquarters team. He was upset about the lack of responsiveness from them. Now, he didn't mention me personally, but I am part of the headquarters team he was referring to. And I reacted. I felt his comments were unfair. I felt the tension in my chest, especially because he said this so publicly.

'Normally I would have said something, and then he would have responded. It would have gone back and forth. But then I looked at the state of heart dashboard in my notebook. Everything was like in slow motion. I became aware of my state of heart.

'I noticed my defensive feelings and thoughts, and I said to myself, "Wait... don't go there. You don't have to. He's in a closed state of heart too... I know the feeling." There was a moment of compassion. It was just a short moment.

'He was watching me, and I guess he anticipated me reacting. Then, as he looked at me, maybe he sensed my calm, and... he changed. His face relaxed and then he said something along the lines of, "I know you all had a lot on your plate as well. And I could have called instead of sending ten reminder emails. And I'm glad you called a meeting, so we could sort things out." The energy in the room changed. We actually had a really productive meeting. And I know it could have gone another way. It felt like a tiny miracle.'

Paul: 'Ah, what a wonderful moment.'

Maryam: 'You see, on the surface of things, nothing has really happened. But a lot has happened inside of me. It was the awareness of my state of heart that helped me navigate this moment.'

Paul: 'I guess so.'

Maryam: 'It's so simple. How could I not have seen this before?'

Paul: 'That is a wonderful question. In order for us to grow, we need not so much to see new things, but to see for ourselves what was always there once we're ready to see it. And there's always more to see. When we transform in that way, the world around us transforms with us.'

'When we transform in that way, the world around us transforms with us.'

Maryam: 'I've just experienced that.'

Paul: 'I think you have. And your experience reminds us that what we can see is a function not so much of our intelligence or knowledge, but of our consciousness, our ability to see ourselves and others from a different vantage point.'

Maryam: 'That would mean that instead of looking primarily to the world around me, I might find even greater leverage inside myself.'

Paul: 'Well, yes. I think so.'

Maryam: 'But then, as a leader, I'm pretty much there to shift things outside of me, am I not?'

Paul: 'You are.'

Maryam: 'Hmmm... that's a bit of a paradox, isn't it?'

Paul: 'How wonderful. Paradoxes can help us see better, so I would suggest we allow it to be what it is and explore a bit more what "focus inside" can look like. Would that work for you?'

Maryam nodded.

Paul: 'So, let me ask you a question. In your meeting, you noticed your state of heart and became more aware of your feelings. Now, given how much they impact on how we experience things around us, have you ever wondered where your feelings come from?'

Maryam: 'I'm not sure. Sometimes, maybe. It's a useful question to ask, because if I knew more about what affects my and others' state of heart, I could leverage that awareness more deliberately and systematically.'

Paul: 'Indeed, you could.'

Maryam: 'So, where do my feelings come from? Well, I guess most of the time it's things that happen to me or people who do something, like having an argument. A piece of news, good or bad, might impact my work.'

Paul: 'I have no doubt you'd react to such news. I'd do that, too.'

Maryam: 'I guess it's more proof we are both alive, right?'

Paul: 'Pretty much so. Now, have you ever been worried about something that then didn't even happen?'

Maryam: 'Oh, yeah, plenty of times.'

Paul: 'OK. And have you ever been upset with someone, or more precisely with something you think they've done, only to later find out they hadn't done it?'

Maryam: 'How did you know? Yes, of course.'

Paul: 'So, if you experienced real feelings, yet the event that you attributed the feelings to never occurred on the surface of this planet, what was it that created those feelings for you? What enabled you to feel what you felt?'

Maryam: 'I've never really thought about that, to be honest. If it wasn't the *events*, it must have been my *mind* that created the feelings. It was my thoughts.'

Paul: 'There is a feeling that comes with every thought. And given that you're always thinking something, you cannot not feel!'

Maryam: 'What do you mean?'

Paul: 'Well, your thoughts are a bit like a movie for your body. Imagine for a moment that you're in a cinema, watching a scary scene in an action movie. How do you feel?'

Maryam: 'Most of the time... scared, of course.'

Paul: 'What do your heart rate and blood pressure do?'

Maryam: 'They go up.'

Paul: 'Now, imagine you're sitting in the same cinema chair with the same people around you, but this time you're watching an inspiring, heart-warming movie. How would you feel?'

Maryam: 'Different. Maybe touched. Or inspired, I guess.'

Paul: 'All that's changed are the pictures and sounds in your mind. Depending on what you watch – the thoughts in your mind – you feel differently, don't you?'

Maryam: 'Hmmm...'

Paul: 'Have you ever watched the famous shower scene in Hitchcock's *Psycho*?'

Maryam: 'Oh, it's been a while. But, yes. What about it?'

Paul: 'Well, think about the scene. Did you ever notice that you actually never see the woman in the shower being stabbed?'

Maryam: 'Hmm, you're right, I think.'

Paul: 'Hitchcock knew that if he let the viewers imagine the murder themselves, it would be more powerful than using special effects and actually showing it. He trusted the power of thought that can create images inside our heads – "image-ination".'

Maryam: 'OK, so our thoughts are like movies in our minds, right?'

Paul: 'Yes. And, more importantly, we can choose the movies we watch. But at times, we don't let go of some movies so easily.'

Maryam: 'Instead, we pay a flat rate and can watch them as much as we like. We can play them again and again, and recreate the feeling every time.'

Paul: 'Flat rate. Did I say I love your humour? Well, it's official now. Yes, we can watch some movies more often than others. Some play the movie called *The World Is Dangerous* more often, while others play the movie *The World Is Abundant*. Now, regardless of the movie you watch, imagine you weren't only seeing 2D or even 3D pictures with your eyes, and hearing the latest Dolby surround sounds with your ears. Imagine you had virtual reality glasses on, and you could also touch and smell the experience.'

Maryam: 'At some stage, I would forget I'm in a movie. It would be my new "reality".'

Paul: 'And your "flat rate" might give you access primarily to the movies you are already aware of versus all the other movies available.'

Maryam: 'What a rip off.'

They laughed.

Maryam: 'OK, I see that much clearer now. My thoughts literally create my feelings. To be honest, I always considered that the events and people around me created my feelings. Don't I react to them too?'

Paul: 'I guess you do. The question is for how long?'

Maryam: 'What do you mean?'

Paul: 'Imagine something happens that causes you to feel stressed or irritated, like an argument with a colleague at work or something of that nature. You probably wouldn't shout, "Hurray", right?'

Maryam: 'Probably not.'

Paul: 'That's understandable, isn't it? We all know this feeling.'

Maryam: 'Oh yes. My heart is bumping, I'm talking to myself, and my chest feels tense.'

Paul: 'And have you ever felt the same way again the next morning, just a few moments after you've woken up?'

Maryam: 'Yes. Sometimes it kicks in under the shower or during breakfast, or when I'm on my way to work...'

Paul: 'So, that's your thoughts going back to work. You see, even when the actual event is long gone, our mind can recreate it. We don't need to relive the event to actually feel it. Our thoughts will let us re-experience it as long as we choose to. Sometimes our mind seems to secretly hope to solve things by going around the racetrack again and again. But the race is over.'

Maryam: 'It's like continuing to experience feelings about a film long after you've left the cinema.'

Paul: 'Yes, that's a great way of putting it. How long the movie will affect you depends on how attached you are to the movie. When you think it's just a movie, it will be just a movie.'

Maryam enjoyed a sip from her coffee as she reflected on what she was learning about the power of her thoughts. 'OK, so however I look at it, it's ultimately my thoughts that create my state of heart, right? That's quite a powerful perspective. It means that I am much more accountable for my own state of heart than I originally thought. And at the same time, I have a lot more power over my state of heart. If I want to shift my feelings, I could...shift my thoughts.'

Paul: 'It's one of the principles that guides effective Chief Energy Officers. For your body, your thoughts are "reality". In other words, your mind and your body are one.'

Maryam: 'I think I'm in the process of discovering a new dimension. I mean, this is really intriguing, but I'm wondering how this relates to daily business. How can I apply this insight into my role as Chief Energy Officer?'

Paul: 'Well, let's see. Can you think of a meeting you're having next week? I mean an important one, where you have skin in the game, the outcome matters, and maybe there's some "history" with the people involved.'

Maryam: 'Oh, there's more than one I can think of. Let me see. There's the one regarding the restructuring of our European organisation. This has been going on for a while, and there's a lot at stake. I'm concerned about us becoming too headquarters focused, and losing touch with our clients. I'm also worried about the tone of these meetings. As a team, we haven't got far yet. And we're under scrutiny from the board – we will need to make a decision soon. I can't share much more, Paul; it's confidential and a bit sensitive.'

Paul: 'Oh, that's fine. How often do you think about this meeting?'

Maryam: 'Almost permanently – when I get up, in the car, in other meetings... it's my way of preparing. I'm thinking about what we need, how some of the team members might react, and how to deal with that.'

Paul: 'Now, would you mind closing your eyes for me so you can better reflect and imagine the meeting?'

Maryam closed her eyes.

Paul: 'Now, just turn your head to the right for a moment. I'd like you to recall the worst moments you've had in these meetings. Imagine the situations and how they felt. Be there again.'

Maryam, after a moment: 'I'm there.'

Paul: 'OK, now I'd like you to think of next week's meeting and image the worst possible outcome. Imagine how the attitudes and actions you've observed in the past will reproduce themselves in this meeting. Imagine how this will impact on the meeting. Just bring that to life, as if you are there now, and let me know when you're there...'

Maryam, after a little while: 'OK, I can see it.'

Paul: 'Now notice how you're feeling. Imagine a whiteboard and write words on it that describe how you feel, OK?'

Maryam, after a moment: 'Alright. Done.'

Paul: 'How would you describe your state of heart?'

Maryam: 'Closed, tense. I'm disappointed.'

Paul: 'Alright. Now, keep your eyes closed, and turn your head to the centre. Let go of what you just thought. Go to the whiteboard and wipe the words off it.'

Maryam: 'OK. Done.'

Paul: 'Thank you. Now turn your head to the left. I'd like you to go back to the meeting, but this time, imagine the best possible outcome. What will be different? What will people say that will make you feel optimistic or energised? What might they do, or not do? How will it feel? Imagine how you would see them if they were loved ones. Accept that they too have a state of heart that changes and lets them see the world in flawed ways at times.'

Maryam: 'I'm working on it... give me a moment... OK, I can see it.'

Paul: 'Alright, now go to the whiteboard again and write down how you're feeling.'

Maryam took a short moment to do this.

Maryam: 'Done. Can I open my eyes?'

Paul: 'Of course, thank you for doing that.'

Maryam: 'That's a strange way of preparing for a meeting.'

Paul: 'What did you notice about the words you wrote on the whiteboard?'

Maryam: 'They were pretty much the same as the words I wrote down the last time we met, when we talked about the state of heart. I could literally feel my heart opening and closing.'

Paul: 'Now let's pause on the first scenario, when you're in a closed state of heart. When you feel that way, how are you most likely to show up in that meeting?'

Maryam: 'I'm not sure, but I guess I'll be tense, paying close attention to how I say things and carefully advocating my view. There might be a few things I'll choose not to share to avoid some undesired reactions – I'll be less open. I believe I will also be less open to what others have to share. I'll make sure others understand me and listen for the views that support my perspective. I might engage less with some people.'

Paul: 'Alright. Thank you, Maryam, for being so open with me. Now, what might the impact of your attitude and feelings be on others, and hence on the meeting, if any?'

Maryam: 'I see your point. Well, I guess it will affect how others react to me, and how they feel. And if others move towards a more closed state of heart, that would impact on what we all say and hear. They might become more cautious and less open too. Then, when we're in that state, we'll all become less collaborative, missing opportunities and ideas.'

Paul: 'And how could that impact on the meeting's outcome, do you think?'

Maryam: 'It could be a bit like the last meeting, which wasn't so productive.'

Paul: 'Now let's turn to the second scenario that you imagined. How did you feel?'

Maryam: 'Well, although I couldn't quite get rid of some thoughts, I was in a more open state of heart. I guess that if I felt that way, I would approach the situation differently.'

Paul: 'For example?'

Maryam: 'For a start, it would be easier for me to see things with more perspective. Whatever solution we come up with, the truth is, it won't be perfect and we'll need to mitigate the caveats anyway. I'd be more inclined to listen for longer, wanting to understand what other people are saying. I might be more vulnerable, truly sharing what's on my mind, and possibly bringing a sense of humour into the equation.'

Paul: 'And how would that be reflected the meeting?'

Maryam: 'Well, I can't predict the future, but I do think we would be more likely to be successful.'

Paul: 'OK, in both instances, when you look back at the results of the meetings, and how you thought about them beforehand, what might you tell yourself afterwards?'

Maryam looked out of the window, not sure what to think. Then she looked at Paul.

Maryam: 'I was right!'

Paul: 'And how might that affect your next conversation?'

Maryam: '... the experience will reaffirm my truth, and so on.' She paused. In her heart she could feel a peaceful sense of clarity that she recognised from other pivotal moments in her life. A sense of awe. 'But then, ultimately, my thoughts will have created the result – my reality.'

Paul looked into her eyes, she looked into his, and they enjoyed the moment. Then Maryam opened her notebook again, drew a circle and showed it to Paul.

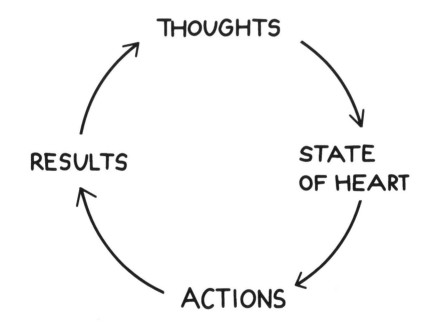

Paul: 'That looks like a great illustration of what we're talking about. What you drew there is what I call the "circle of energy".'

Maryam: 'Why do you call it that?'

Paul: 'Because it reminds me that tangible forms of energy – things we can see, feel, hear or touch – are ultimately rooted in less tangible forms of energy like our thoughts – electrons floating back and forth between synapses. All human creation starts with a thought.'

Maryam: 'Hmm. I'm thinking that if I choose to look at the events we talked about this way, I could quite literally influence the outcome I'm likely to get by shifting the way I think about things or people.'

Paul: 'Well, in my experience, that's where I have the highest leverage, because it's indeed my thinking that creates my reality, and because I always have the power to shift my own thinking – regardless of circumstance.'

Maryam: 'Provided, of course, you're aware of it. Then, with awareness...'

Paul: '...comes choice.'

Maryam: 'So, I need to study psychology or hire an experienced coach to shadow me all day?'

Paul, laughing: 'Well, I can see value in both. Hmm... let me ask you this. If you look at your state of heart, when do you tend to be a more effective problem solver, in open or closed states?'

Maryam: 'Most of the time when I'm in open ones, I'd say.'

Paul: 'OK, and when do you tend to deal more effectively with stress or challenges that life puts in front of you?'

Maryam: 'When I'm in more open states.'

Paul: 'When do you tend to naturally be a more effective parent, team member, and leader?'

Maryam: 'OK, I see. I tend to act more effectively when I'm in an open state of heart. It's the circle of energy, right?'

Paul: 'Indeed. But why? Do you mind if I make a little addition to your drawing?'

Maryam: 'Of course not.'

Paul took Maryam's pen and added an arrow pointing from 'state of heart' to 'thought'.

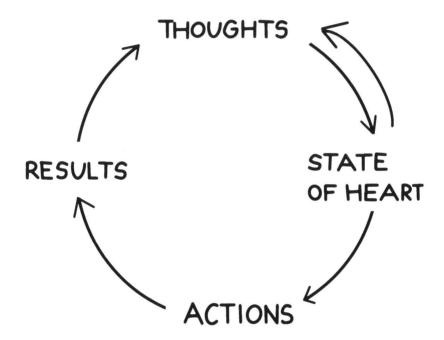

Maryam: 'If my feelings, my state of heart, are the result of my thoughts, then vice versa, my state of heart will also reflect...'

Paul: '...the quality of your thoughts. You see, sometimes we look at our feelings as an accurate indicator of our reality, ie what other people do or say or the things that happen. We tend to say, "I feel this way because this and that happened". And there's some truth in that, of course, but a more complete picture of what's going on is that your feelings are not so much an indicator of the events around you, but what you choose to think about them. Two people in front of the same situation will experience different emotions...'

Maryam: '... because they think differently about it.' She reflected for a moment and then continued. 'So, if I use our analogy of a car, seeing my state of heart tells me something about what is going on inside my car – that is my brain, my thinking process – but it doesn't tell me a lot about the traffic or weather conditions.'

Paul: 'Indeed. Now, you are more likely to get an overheated engine in a traffic jam in the summer, but it's still been your choice not to give your engine a break, even knowing about the hot temperature.'

Maryam: 'So, I can not only leverage my thoughts to influence my state of heart, I can also use my state of heart as an indicator of the kind of thoughts I'm producing. And with awareness...'

Paul: '...comes choice.' He smiled. 'Indeed. Very simply, I've learned that I can rely on my thinking and feelings when my heart is open. I can't rely on my feelings and thoughts so much when my heart is closed. It's not the wisdom of my heart talking. The door is closed. When I'm in a more closed state of heart, it has served me well to hold my thoughts more lightly.'

Maryam: 'What do you mean by "holding your thoughts lightly"?'

Paul: 'Well, knowing that my thinking is probably more biased than usual, more extreme, more flawed, I can choose not to pay much attention to what my inner voice is telling me, or not to say what I feel like saying, or not to take the decision it's suggesting to me.'

Maryam: 'So you're using your state of heart to make decisions?'

Paul: 'Oh yes.'

Maryam: 'But shouldn't we remove our emotions from business so we can make rational, fact-based decisions?'

Paul: 'I believe thoughts and feelings are two universal tools that enable us to make sense of what we perceive with our senses. I don't see value in throwing either of them away, and as our conversation has shown, they are intimately interdependent. When you're in an open state of heart, you might use the data your senses perceive correctly. It seems to me we must learn over time to leverage both for making judgments.'

Maryam: 'OK, I can see that, but there are facts we need to work with. For example, either something is profitable or it isn't, either someone gets a result or they don't, right? Not everything is a matter of perspective.'

'Don't trust your feelings and thoughts when your heart is closed. It's not the wisdom of your heart talking. The door is closed.'

Paul: 'I believe you're right. And most of the time, people don't even disagree on the facts, but on the *meaning* of the facts and their *implications*. In our restaurant, when it comes to planning schedules or how much we need to purchase, where we need to invest, where we need to make savings, how we can improve a process, my team and I look first at the data we have to inform our choices. It's both necessary and helpful, I find. And we're asking ourselves the question, "Does that make sense?" It's a question for our intellect, and it typically brings us some helpful answers. But then there are questions where looking at pros and cons or facts and figures alone doesn't seem to offer an answer. Can you think of areas like that in your part of the business?'

Maryam: 'Oh, plenty, especially the questions related to people's development – things that are uncertain or where we need to try things we have little or no experience in. Looking at it from this perspective, I'd say they are the majority of business challenges.'

Paul: 'In those instances, I still ask, "Does it make sense?" That alone can give you the answer to many relatively simple questions. For others, it can be a good starting point. I'm not suggesting you ignore the answer; it's just incomplete. I would also ask, "Does it feel right?" I'm asking my intuition or my heart, if you like. If it doesn't feel right then I won't do it. I will pause.'

Maryam: 'So, what I feel is data too, right?'

Paul: 'Yes, that's how I see it. I'm using all the information available to me, using my whole being, rather than restricting myself. Albert Einstein said, "We should take care not to make intellect our God. It has, of course, powerful muscles, but no personality. It cannot lead, it can only serve." Our thoughts serve us best when we are in an open state of heart.'

Maryam opened her notebook and added another arrow to the circle of energy.

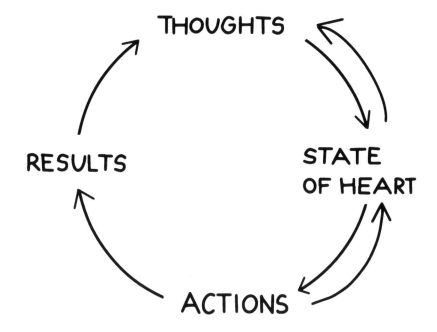

Paul: 'Now, here's the caveat. When I'm in closed states of heart, my thinking, the voice inside my head, tends to be at its loudest and most assertive. Alternatively, when I'm in more open states of heart, this voice tends to be quiet and easy to overlook. Does that resonate with your own experience?'

Maryam: 'Oh yes, I often feel that. When I'm upset, it comes with a sense of self-righteousness. Things appear to be more black and white and less nuanced. It's easy for me to justify whatever I do, like getting louder, or a being a bit condescending, or using various subtle tactics to coerce others... or convince myself into doing what doesn't feel right. I might even slightly exaggerate some events, hoping this will get me what I want. I can see myself doing that when I'm with my children, with colleagues, or on the phone with complete strangers in a call centre.'

Paul: 'Maryam, I appreciate you being so open and vulnerable about this. I can relate to many things you have shared.'

Maryam, with a sassy smile: 'Well, it's good to know that I'm in good company.'

Paul: 'If you consider the problems we have at work, which are typically about someone or something, they all happen in our minds. What we label as "problems" are actually often situations seen from a closed state of heart. If we see them from a more open state of heart, new possibilities can occur that were invisible before.'

Maryam: 'At times, when we're stuck, our attention might then be better invested in shifting our state of heart than in trying to "solve the problem" with our mind.'

Paul: 'Then we will think and see differently, creating different outcomes.'

Maryam: 'Do you have an example that comes to mind?'

Paul: 'Let me think. Imagine you are disagreeing about a decision with someone else.'

Maryam: 'Yes...'

Paul: 'If one of you is feeling worried or anxious, or you're both feeling like that, you're unlikely to have enough compassion to truly listen to each other, enough perspective to see each other. It's unlikely you will have a helpful conversation to find a solution – whatever someone is proposing will look dangerous or problematic. Your mind will literally produce thoughts that are defensive. As a result, you might talk defensively, impacting on the state of heart of your colleague.'

Maryam: 'I can picture that feeling.'

Paul: 'When my wife and I are in a closed state of heart, we can strongly disagree about how the plates are supposed to fit into the dishwasher. When we are in an open state of heart, we are able to talk about even difficult questions that have no obvious answers to them, and are more likely to move forward. Then we find the beginnings of solutions that we couldn't see before.'

Maryam: 'That's interesting. Usually when my state of heart is closed, I tend to focus even more on the *content* of an argument, on convincing the other person of my point of view. I hadn't really considered that my irritation might itself be nurturing the problem as it presents itself.'

Paul: 'Let me ask you this. Have you ever experienced a time when you were looking for a solution, and you were thinking hard about it, but couldn't quite nail it? And then at a later time, the solution or idea you were looking for came along? I mean, all of a sudden you just knew?'

Maryam: 'Yes, many times.'

Paul: 'When did the solution come?'

Maryam: 'While I was driving the car, showering, often first thing in the morning or when I went to bed, sometimes while walking the dogs.'

Paul: 'Would it be fair to say that these are moments when you have stopped thinking hard?'

Maryam: 'Yes, sort of.'

Paul: 'That's when your quiet voice – some call it intuition – can be heard, because there's less noise. It's a very smart voice, but a quiet one. When you're in a closed state of heart, when you have a rock band playing in your brain, you tend not to hear it. When you're quiet, what you're looking for can come to you.'

Maryam looked at Paul, noticing that she felt more peaceful than usual. Her heart felt wide open.

Maryam: 'Paul, I don't know how to say this. I really enjoy our conversations, yet I somehow think it's not so much what we're talking about. Don't get me wrong – I'm truly benefitting from these reflections with you. But I sense that what I'm really enjoying is your presence. I feel so... so human when I'm with you. It's not what you say, but how you are that is somehow touching me. I'm not sure if I'm making any sense here.'

Paul: 'A lot of sense, Maryam. Thank you.'

Paul and Maryam stood up and grabbed each other's hands, pressing them together gently, like parents holding on to their children. They looked into each other's eyes; they needed no words to express their gratitude to one another. Both felt alive. Just alive.

They agreed to meet the following week.

Paul: 'Have a wonderful weekend, Maryam. Thank you for today.'

Maryam: 'You too. Thank you, Paul.'

Journaling

It wasn't until the next day that Maryam had chance to look back at her dialogue with Paul.

In the morning she gave George a lift to the airport, and on her way back she ran some errands.

When she arrived home the weather was simply beautiful, and she felt a lack of daylight and fresh air so she decided to go for a walk outside and enjoy what the day had to offer. As she was walking through her favourite park, she allowed her mind to wander. She enjoyed contemplating this way. Often she felt, when walking this way, that she didn't have to find clarity. Rather, clarity would come to her.

When she arrived back home she felt energised and alive. She grabbed her journal, and simply jotted down the thoughts that had come to her during her walk and in the moment:

- There is a feeling that comes with every thought. Feelings are the body's reactions to our thoughts. Thoughts are my body's reality.

- And, vice versa, different feelings, different states of heart, produce different types of thoughts. My body and my mind truly are one. In fact, they have never been separate in the first place.

- 'Problems' are often situations, seen from a closed state of heart. Sometimes my attention might be better invested in asking how I can shift my own or other's state of heart, rather than in trying to 'solve the problem'.

- My 'reality' is like a permanent 4D movie with sensory effects – only that I've forgotten that I'm actually in a movie theatre. I have the power to choose which movie I watch… what I focus my thoughts on.

- My heart provides data for decision making. I can listen to the intelligence of my intellect by asking, 'Does it make sense?' I tap into the intelligence of my heart, my intuition, by asking, 'How does that feel?'

- However, the wisdom of my heart whispers, it's hard to hear in closed states of heart when I have a rock band playing in my mind.

- I can rely on my thoughts when I'm in open states of heart. Let me hold my thoughts more lightly when in more closed states of heart.

Maryam paused, and then added one more note:

- I grow, less by seeing new things, than by seeing differently. Strangely, the world around me changes as I am changing myself.

CHAPTER 4

High Energy Mindsets: Non-Judgmental Judgment

'Watch your thoughts; they become words.
Watch your words; they become actions.
Watch your actions; they become habits.
Watch your habits; they become character.
Watch your character; it becomes your destiny.'

Lao Tzu

'The eye is the lamp of the body. So, if your eye
is healthy, your whole body will be full of light.'

Matthew 6:22

Paul and Maryam met in the afternoon a week later. The restaurant had closed after lunch, and Paul's team had already left for the weekend. A soothing quietness replaced the buzz that so often filled the space.

Maryam had just returned from a week of business travel. She stopped by her office to drop off a few folders before walking over to the restaurant to meet with Paul. It was sunny outside, there was a gentle breeze, and Maryam enjoyed the smell of freshly cut grass it carried. It was the first time she'd noticed this particular scent, signalling the arrival of spring. She noticed the sound of a distant lawnmower and a few snowdrops sticking their heads out next to the pathway.

Closing her eyes, she stopped for a moment and took a deep breath, silently hoping she could capture a bit of the joyful energy and vibrancy of spring. As she felt the sun warming her face, Maryam realised it had been a while since she'd been out in natural surroundings, and decided to ask her husband and kids to go for a walk all together this afternoon.

She entered the restaurant building and spotted Paul, who was closing the main gate.

Maryam: 'Hello, Paul, how are you?'

Paul: 'Hello, Maryam, I'm very well. Good to see you. And yourself?'

Maryam: 'I've just come back from a few days of travel and realised I'm really missing fresh air and daylight. It's wonderful outside. Shall we walk in the park?'

Paul: 'Ah, yes, that's a wonderful idea. The restaurant is closed anyway and a few breaths of fresh air would do me a lot of good too. It's been a busy week. Let's have a walking meeting, shall we?'

Maryam left her luggage in Paul's office and they walked towards the park, which was only a few steps away.

Paul: 'Ah, you were right, Maryam. It's beautiful outside.'

They strolled for a few moments in silence, realising how much they'd started to enjoy one another's company. They didn't require words to say it. Walking together was both the source of this shared joy and its expression.

Paul: 'So, tell me, how has your week been?'

Maryam: 'It's been a good week, thank you. Our conversations and reflections helped me a lot. I've kind of started observing the circle of energy in action, in myself, and during meetings with colleagues and clients.

'In one instance, I felt nervous before a meeting. Given that the meeting hadn't even taken place yet, I reminded myself that it could only be my thoughts about it that were making me feel this way. I decided to write down those thoughts running through my mind. I didn't dismiss them, but folded the sheet of paper and chose to hold the thoughts more lightly, telling myself, "And it could all be different." Then I closed my eyes and imagined the outcome I was hoping for and how I wanted to show up. I imagined how I would like to feel in that moment'

Paul: 'That's interesting. And how did that go for you?'

Maryam: 'Well, I must admit the meeting was certainly much more constructive than I had anticipated. Sure, there was some tension at the start. That was to be expected, and I noticed my heart closing a little. Yet as I was choosing to keep it open – I don't know how to say it otherwise – I realised how my colleague, who I had been so concerned about, opened up. He kind of softened. Our meeting took on a different quality, a different energy. We were starting to think together, rather than trying to convince each other of our respective views, if you see what I mean.'

Paul: 'Oh, yes.'

Maryam: 'Now, to be clear, we still have a lot more to talk about. Yet I sense there is more trust now to build on, and a better foundation on which to move forward. He accompanied me to the exit, which he had never done before, and shared with me how much he valued the conversation we'd had. Maybe we all just had a good day?'

Paul: 'Maybe. And maybe you helped it to become one through the presence and energy you brought to the moment. In any case, I'm glad for you. What else have you noticed?'

Maryam: 'I've started paying more attention to my state of heart. Not all the time, but more often I can sense my heart opening and closing. And more often, when I've realised I'm beginning to be in a more closed state of heart, I've chosen to wait before saying something, or reacting or deciding. I haven't wanted my autopilot to be in charge then. And sometimes, I admit, when I've been in a closed state of heart, I've gone ahead and said what I felt like saying anyway...'

Maryam looked at Paul and continued with a wink of her eye. '... because I can, if you see what I mean.'

Paul: 'You are not alone, I do that too. We're all members of the same species, aren't we?'

Maryam and Paul enjoyed it when they allowed themselves to be a bit silly.

Maryam: 'I have also noticed how I'm more acutely aware of the energy in the room when I pay deliberate attention to it. I notice how it's shifting during conversations because of the tone of someone's voice or a small gesture or facial expression. I then feel the desire to transform that energy, yet quite frankly, I don't always know how.'

Paul: 'That makes all the sense in the world to me. Well, tell me more... what did you try?'

Maryam: 'I can't tell you exactly what I've done, but holding on to my firm intention of wanting to nurture a healthy energy seems to have helped me. Sometimes it's been a smile, sometimes the choice or the tone of my own words. Sometimes it's helped to listen for a little longer, wanting to understand and dial down my habitual urge to advise or react. When I've done this, after a short moment, I've noticed my heart opening again. I'm not sure if it's always something I've consciously done, you know? I have just been aware.'

Paul: 'Maryam, thank you for sharing that. It's a great insight. You see, the energy in a room cannot be separated from your own presence. Do you remember what you shared with me when I left your office last week?'

Maryam: 'Yes of course. I told you how your presence touched me.'

Paul: 'And so do you affect me. You can't not affect others, because we are all connected. More and more I've come to realise that it's less the *situation* that creates my energy, and more my *energy* that creates the situation. I seem to have the most influence on the energy in a situation, and hence the outcome, by attending to my own state of heart.'

Maryam: 'You mean how you feel will genuinely affect others in the room?'

Paul: 'Oh yes, it's that simple. It's a well-known scientific fact that moods

> 'More and more I've come to realise that it's less the *situation* that creates my energy, and more my *energy* that creates the situation.'

spread quickly. I mean faster than words. It's a survival mechanism – we humans had to communicate with each other before we used words. We did and still do that very effectively through expressing and creating feelings.

'If we were in danger, you would be able to see the anxiety in my face and feel it yourself before you heard me shouting, "Sabre-toothed tiger coming – run." And you would react to it and run because you would be able to remember the feeling of being attacked. You don't need to recall the details and special circumstances of the previous attack; all you needed to know – to feel – is "this is dangerous". That feeling is still in play. So your presence affects others, whether you want it to or not.'

Maryam: 'So, when people are thinking or talking in my presence, much of it is a reflection of how they are feeling because of my presence. They are not entirely separate from me.'

Paul: 'That awareness is I think, at the very heart of being an effective Chief Energy Officer, because shifting your own state of heart is one of the most effective ways of shifting the feelings of others.'

Maryam: 'I'm glad you're sharing that with me, Paul, because I was thinking about something related to that this past week.'

Paul: 'Please tell me more about it.'

Maryam: 'Well, on the plane, I was wondering that if it's thoughts that affect my state of heart, and that of others, what kind of thoughts could help me to be in an open state of heart more often, more deliberately,

'So, when people are thinking or talking in my presence, much of it is a reflection of how they are feeling because of my presence.'

and to reconnect with such a state when I'm not there anymore. I mean, what else can I do to put the circle of energy into action?'

Paul: 'Oh, that's a wonderful question. Well, from my point of view, there are a few specific mindsets that tend to help me and the team to keep perspective more often.'

Mindsets

Maryam: 'I would love to hear about them. Before you go there, though, you just used the word mindset. Is that different from thought?'

Paul: 'Oh, thanks for asking. Well, they are related. You see, thoughts come and go. You are always thinking something. In other words, since you were born, you have been trying to make sense of the world around you, right?'

Maryam, smiling: 'Yes, I think so.'

Paul: 'Now, at some stage, you have experienced – consciously or not – or others have told you that some behaviours get you the results you wish for, and some help you avoid the results you don't want, like pain.'

Maryam: 'That's called learning.'

Paul: 'Yeah. Now, just like you don't really think about how you change gears in a car – you *are* thinking, just not so consciously – you've developed loosely held groups of thoughts that help you navigate through life. If something works once, you've probably tried it again. If it works a third time, it looks like a recipe for success.'

Maryam: 'The same is probably true when things don't work or you don't appreciate the results.'

Paul: 'Unlike the thousands of thoughts that come and go, these loosely held groups remain. They become filters, like on a camera through which you look at whatever might happen.'

Maryam: 'That's what you refer to as mindsets'

Paul: 'Yes. Your mind is "set" that way. There's nothing wrong with it. Mindsets are a necessity of life, but most of them are so habitual that you can't see them anymore. They are like water to a fish – they impact on all you do, yet you are unaware of what they do. Most of the time, you only notice them when someone else holds a different mindset, or when you reflect on recurring patterns in your life. Mindsets are the autopilot you've just mentioned. Again, they are not good or bad. You need them, and with awareness...'

Maryam: '... comes choice.'

Paul: 'And, of course, although they are intangible, mindsets provide great leverage for tangible change, as they affect not only one, but many situations.'

Maryam: 'Do you have an example, Paul?'

Paul: 'Hmm, let me think...'

They stopped walking for a moment and looked over the city.

Paul: 'One mindset that I became aware of a while ago is what I now call "leadership by discontentment". Once I could see it, I realised how that mindset affected how I conducted myself as a parent, a leader and even as a husband. I first started to just notice it when it kicked in. Then, over time, I changed my mindset, and as a result changed both how I felt and how I behaved. And with that, the world around me changed as well. Let me explain.'

Maryam: 'Please.'

Paul: 'Let's say my son didn't clean up his room, although earlier that day he'd promised me he would.'

Maryam: 'I can picture that very well.'

Paul: 'Most of the time, I would get upset and angry, especially if he had done this repeatedly. My tone of voice, my whole body and my words would tell him, "I am angry because you disappointed me, because you let me down." In my mind, I more or less secretly wished that making him feel guilty and ashamed – for not having cleaned up his room and, as a result, for making me suffer – would make him change his behaviour. I also convinced myself that he needed to experience how his actions made others feel so that he could learn to act more responsibly moving forward. In a sense, I told myself that *not* showing my anger, holding it back, would be disingenuous – isn't anger the natural reaction to disobedience? I even felt doing so would be irresponsible – other people wouldn't look at him with as much goodwill as I did. It all made sense.'

Maryam: 'I have certainly thought and felt what you are describing.'

Paul: 'It was only after many of these instances that I realised what he was actually learning from experiencing me this way was that there is only one possible emotional answer to obstacles: anger and discontentment. I could also choose for him to experience – and hence learn – that he always has *emotional choices* and hence *power* when he's confronted with results he doesn't like or agree with.'

There was a moment of silence, allowing the thought to unfold.

Paul: 'But first, I needed to accept that I had a choice myself to feel that way. Until then, because of my mindset, I felt *genuinely* disappointed, because he could have avoided me feeling this way if only he had cleaned up his room. Again, it all made sense. And it worked, at home and at work.'

Maryam: 'What do you mean?'

Paul: 'Well, people *would* do what I'd hoped they'd do as a result. In this instance, my son would clean up his room – with his head down, but he'd do it. He had no choice. And although I expressed my discontentment in a more socially acceptable – or, as I thought, "smarter" – way in front of my employees, by taking a deep breath, rolling my eyes, or asking in an irritated voice, "Why didn't you check these facts beforehand?', I still wanted my feelings to be known. I knew, somewhere inside of me, that doing so would trigger feelings of inadequacy in them, and they would then go and do what I wanted to reduce the pain of that feeling. It works. That reinforced my mindset – not consciously, but fundamentally. I would think, *There you go, why did we have to go through that?*'

Maryam: 'Knowing you now makes it kind of hard to believe that you used to think and act in this way. I'm experiencing you differently. You must have changed quite a lot. What made you become aware of your own mindset?'

Paul: 'Your observation is pointing to the heart of mindsets. I had an insight that transformed my mindset. Once I had that insight – a realisation from the inside – my mindset started shifting. And it stuck. You can't take away an insight. Once it is there, it unfolds its power – gently, but steadily. I was watching the same people, and nothing had changed outside of me, but I was seeing something different.'

Maryam: 'What happened?'

Paul: 'Well, since we are kind of caught in our own mindsets, where everything we do makes sense, sometimes we need an outside perspective coming from a place of goodwill, or a question that doesn't quite fit our existing mindset, to help us open a window and look outside. It was both in my case.

'At first, I noticed that my son would anticipate how I'd feel. He'd say, "Dad, don't get upset, please, OK? I haven't cleaned up my room yet, but..." I also noticed that he was often upset with himself when he felt he was being treated unfairly, to which, of course, I reacted.

'My employees would often add a preamble to things and say, "OK, Paul, you might not like this, but let me explain..." And I could feel they were also being less open and holding back. You see, both my team and my son were simply afraid of, and hence trying to avoid, a reaction from me that would cause the feeling they didn't want to experience. Instead of making them powerful, I was weakening them. But I couldn't see that at the time. On the contrary, I felt judged – I hadn't said a thing, and they'd told me how I was likely to react. It felt like a verdict in *The Minority Report* for something that hadn't happened yet.'

They walked for a moment in silence. Then Paul continued.

'One evening I was talking about what I was experiencing at home and at work with a dear friend, hoping to gain some consolation from him. After listening to me for quite a while, he shared something he had learned with me.'

Maryam: 'And what was that?'

Paul: 'He said, "You're right, Paul." And then he added, "No one can upset you - *without* your permission."'

Maryam: 'Hmm...'

Paul: 'What he said puzzled me; it made me wonder. I started to see something that had always been there before me, but was still invisible – it was my own *mindset*.

'That evening, we explored why getting upset made sense to me. He didn't judge me; he simply helped me reflect and work through that question for myself. As I was talking with him, my mindset emerged in front of me as clearly as if it was a third person in the room. It was not about seeing what was "right" or "wrong" with it. Simply, instead of looking *through* it, I looked *at* it. By examining it, I could see the construct of it, how it supported itself and co-created life as I experienced it.

'For example, it is human to feel disappointed. However, there is no physical law to say that I had to feel this way. It was my emotional autopilot. Like any emotion, anger is a learned behaviour. And as such, it can be unlearned. I had bought into the belief that I *had* to be upset.'

They walked a few steps before Paul continued.

'It then dawned on me that there also was a feeling of vulnerability inside me. It was quieter, less obvious, and came from me feeling embarrassed at being seen this way. While I wanted others to feel my disappointment, at the same time, I didn't want to be seen as an easily upset person. So, I justified my feelings, like that government spokesperson we talked about.'

Maryam: 'I remember, using intellect to justify their decisions.'

Paul: 'My friend also helped me see some blind spots. While it was undeniable that my son and my team were mostly doing what

I hoped they'd do, I was paying a price. By coercing them, fundamentally, with different degrees of fear, I'd made sure their hearts closed. And you know how we are in those closed states of heart. I lost their energy – or engagement, if you like. The best I could get was some sort of compliance. And my son wasn't complying because he cared about his room, he just didn't want me to get mad. I could sense that. Yet seen through my mindset, rather than prompting me to question my involvement in the situation, it strengthened my view that "he hadn't quite learned his lesson yet".'

Paul paused for a moment. 'Does that give you a sense of what a mindset can look like and how powerful it is?'

Maryam: 'Oh yes. I appreciate that you are willing to share such a personal example of what you've learned about yourself. Your mindset created its own reality. It's an example of the circle of energy, right? Our mindsets are not just an *interpretation* of our so-called reality – they are *creators* of reality.'

Paul: 'Yes, and normally thoughts just come and go. When I looked at my son's room and said to myself, "He didn't clean it up – again", that was only a thought. But thoughts can turn into mindsets when we think them more regularly. Mindsets are more solid and a bit more tangible. You could talk about them or write them down once you become aware of them. As a result, they feel more real, like my mindset of "anger is necessary". Sometimes mindsets can even turn into beliefs. They become solid personal truths and permanent tenants of your mind; you become attached to them. Then they don't just come and go – unless you end the contract. I had created a belief when I moved to "he has to experience my anger, or he will have trouble later in life".'

Maryam: 'I see. Now, in the light of our circle of energy, I'd guess that the stronger the thought, the stronger the feeling that goes with it.'

Paul: 'Yes. You might hear yourself saying, "I feel strongly about it". Now, feelings are more tangible or real than thoughts. You can experience them and see them in others; you can even measure them. Your body releases chemicals that affect it physically: your heart reacts, your blood pressure rises, and your muscles tense. Your feelings make your thoughts seem real to you.'

Maryam: 'OK. And then, as a result, you say or do something.'

Paul: 'And that's even more tangible. Your words and actions physically affect people and situations. Your thought has turned into a material reality.'

Maryam: 'And finally, like in your example, the outcome has an impact on your mindset. Material reality becomes less tangible again, while your mindset actually becomes stronger with every iteration.'

Maryam and Paul walked in front of a bank with a wonderful view over hills and meadows, where some of the first blossom was coating the trees, filling their eyes with enlivening, fresh colours.

Maryam: 'Paul – do you mind if we sit down for a moment? I would like to add some thoughts to my notes.'

Paul: 'Oh, not at all. This seems like a perfect spot.'

The two sat on the bank. Paul enjoyed the view, and Maryam took out her notebook and looked for the page where she had drawn the circle of energy. She scribbled a few additional notes next to it to capture insights that she wanted to reflect on.

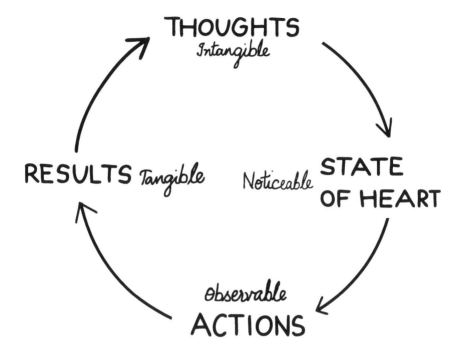

Maryam: 'Paul, thank you. I'm glad we've stepped back a bit and discussed mindsets. I sense there is no such thing as a right or wrong mindset. However, when we want different outcomes, we will need to focus our attention on where it has the most leverage, and that's inside.'

Paul: 'There is value, of course, to looking at outcomes and behaviours too, as long as we keep sight of the fact that these are, to a large extent, related to our thoughts. It's like the old joke about the drunken man who's looking for his lost keys under a streetlamp. A police officer walks by and asks him why he is looking under the lamp and not in his pockets. The drunk responds, "Because there is more light here."'

High-frequency mindsets

Maryam: 'I'm thinking about your team. There seems to be something that unites them, something they share that keeps them in a good place in spite of the time pressure and stress that they must be experiencing. I'm not sure how to say it – I'm wondering if there are a few *shared* mindsets you and your team nurture. Are there some mindsets that have helped you over the years to access your open states of heart more often, regardless of circumstances? Are there specific mindsets that have helped you deal with daily business needs, such as making decisions in the light of uncertainty, complexity and constraints of time, budget, and procedures? You know – the normal challenging stuff. If there are, would there be any that you would single out?'

Paul looked at Maryam and nodded. They waited a bit for the question to do its work and allow thoughts to occur in Paul's mind, coming from an open, inspired heart.

Paul: 'These are pertinent questions and I'm glad you're asking me to reflect on them and share with you what I see. At the beginning, when we were struggling to turn our business around, we actually talked about mindsets and the role of the state of heart. It was unusual and new to all of us, and it felt a bit uncomfortable. But if mindsets could help us create the organisation we wanted, it made sense to reflect on the way we were thinking and feeling and our state of heart at work.'

Maryam: 'That's what I'm wondering about.'

Paul: 'Since then, we've been having regular conversations just like the one you and I are having at the moment. Given that our minds are always thinking something, it has made increasing sense to us to explore whether there are certain mindsets prevalent in all of us in moments when we are at our best, in spite of challenging circumstances. We were wondering if there were any shared mindsets which we could then deliberately tap into to stay more often in open states of heart. As we have shared our life experiences, we've realised that we are our best selves when our minds are *suspending our habitual judgment of ourselves, others, ideas, and life situations*, or at least are less attached to these judgments.'

Maryam: 'Hmm, that sounds interesting. But isn't business all about making judgments – predominantly the right ones, if possible?'

Paul: 'Yes, you're right. We indeed constantly need to make judgments to take actions. The majority of our thoughts are probably judgments, helping us to make choices. But let me ask you – have you ever found yourself in front of situations where no "answers" or "solutions" arise from your past experience?'

Maryam: 'Oh yes. That's rather more the norm than the exception.'

Paul: 'And have you ever taken decisions when your heart was closed that you later regretted, mumbling to yourself, "I knew it," and wondering why you didn't go with your "inner voice" in the first place?'

Maryam: 'Ahh, yes. That's happened in my life. We spoke about the inner voice last week, didn't we?'

Paul: 'Yes, we did. And have you ever made a decision, or made what we call a "gut choice", that felt good, even though you didn't have enough data to support your decision, and it ended up being a wise move?'

> 'We are our best selves when our minds are suspending our habitual judgment of ourselves, others, ideas, and life situations.'

Maryam: 'Of course. That happens too.'

Paul: 'You see, there is nothing wrong with judgment as such. It's necessary – we need to make judgment calls. And your state of heart will tell you if you're making that choice through a curious or a judgmental filter.'

Maryam reflected. 'Open hearts make judgment calls – closed hearts judge.'

Paul: 'Ah yes, you could say it that way. I love that. Looks like I will quote you to my team again. You see, as a team, we've tried to become more mindful observers, if you like, of the *feelings* that come with our thoughts, and the *process* of our own thinking. For example, how thoughts become beliefs. And we've experienced how that has helped us to still have our views – strong ones at times – yet hold them more lightly. This leaves space for new, often better, thoughts or judgments that we would probably not have seen otherwise.'

Maryam: 'Strong views, lightly held. I like that.'

Paul: 'We sometimes call it non-judgmental judgment, and it's the foundation of the four mindsets – the four dimensions that help us be at our best.'

Maryam: 'How we look at ourselves, others, ideas, and life situations, right?'

Paul: 'Yes.'

Maryam: 'It would be great to explore these.'

Paul: 'OK, let's start with how we view ourselves. I'd like to say, though,

'Open hearts make judgment calls - closed hearts judge.'

that these four dimensions are not separate, just different aspects of the same notion. They all help me personally to stay in an open state of heart, or revert there more quickly when I'm not. For me, they are simply different doors to the same living room.'

Suspending judgment of self: the door to our innate health

Paul: 'Maryam, have you ever had an argument with someone?'

Maryam, hesitating a bit: 'Well yes, of course, plenty of times. Even with those I love... *especially* with those I love.'

Paul, laughing light-heartedly: 'You're not alone. Now, how do you tend to feel when you are in the middle of such an argument?'

Maryam: 'In hindsight, I'd say I feel self-righteous, like I have to win. And I'm pretty good at making my case, if you see what I mean. I can be very intense.'

Paul: 'Yes, I see. And have you ever left an argument in despair, not seeing a way out, or with a sense of resentment? And then, after a night's sleep, you have woken up and not felt that intensity anymore? You didn't feel the anger anymore, even though you kind of tried to?'

Maryam: 'Oh yes, often. I might not even be sure why it all started in the first place.'

Paul: 'So, your state of heart has changed – your heart has opened, and it did so without you doing anything in particular, right?'

Maryam: 'Yes, I think that's right.'

Paul: 'So, if you think about that, you can rest assured of two things. First of all, you're always feeling something. Second, whatever you're feeling right now will change – with or without your making. You see, it's like the weather. When there's rain, you find shelter somewhere and wait for it to pass. That only makes sense because you know for a fact that the rain *will* pass in the near future, unless you're in a country with a monsoon season. Then it might take a bit longer. *Knowing* that it will pass gives you peace of mind. You don't get attached to it. Now, the same is true for your state of heart – whatever you're feeling now, you can trust that your feelings will change. Have you experienced that?'

Maryam: 'I like your analogy, Paul. Yes, of course, I can think of many instances where I've ended up in a closed state of heart, and then, the next day, kind of overnight, it had changed.'

Paul: 'Alright. Now, when I remind myself that my state of heart is only *temporary*, ephemeral by nature, I often find this awareness itself helps me revert to a more open state of heart more quickly. The pain I experience in a closed state of heart doesn't come so much from the *feeling* itself, but from my attempt to *suppress* that feeling, from not accepting it. In a sense, that's like not accepting rain. In my experience, acceptance is a major attribute of resilient hearts, and you'll find that for the other three dimensions too.'

Maryam remained quiet for a moment. 'I haven't really looked at it that way. So far, I've always considered that I had to *do* something about my feeling – that if I was in a closed state of heart, something was wrong with me. I guess that as a result of that mindset, I rejected some of the feelings I was experiencing, telling myself, "Maryam, you're not supposed to be upset." I didn't consider that rejecting or trying to fix a closed state of heart might nurture it even more.'

Paul took a few contemplative breaths, allowing his thoughts to unfold and new thoughts to emerge. Then he continued.

'Strangely, it often seems to be the judgment of our feelings that hurts more than the actual feelings. Now, acceptance is not the same as indifference or apathy. When you are accepting, you are choosing to be aware of your state of heart, but you don't judge it. Acceptance means not wasting energy on what's already present anyway; it's choosing not to fight, but embrace life by surrendering to it. Coming from that stance, if you accept painful feelings, you become more immune to their pain.'

Maryam: 'I can see that.'

Paul: 'A dear friend of mine once shared the beginning of a poem with me, written by Fabienne Cuisinier. I use this poem to help me remain in a state of curious acceptance, not indifference, when it comes to how I look at myself. She reminded me that I am "Perfectly perfect with all my imperfections".'

PERFECT

Maryam: 'I really am starting to like these paradoxes. Seen from that mindset, myself and other people are not "problems to be solved".[1] I can grow without self-judgment. And I couldn't grow without imperfections.'

Paul: 'Now, imagine what that mindset, that "come-from", can do for how you look at yourself and how you look at others.'

---

[1] I attribute this saying to Ann Clancy, co-author of *Appreciative Coaching – A Positive Process for Change*, from whom I've learned not to look at people as 'problems to be solved', but 'mysteries to be appreciated'.

Mariam: 'It nurtures compassion for self and others. At the same time, it reduces rejection of self and others. It... it heals.'

Paul and Maryam took a few breaths to enjoy the thoughts that had surfaced during their conversation, as well as the peaceful energy that seemed to come with them.

Paul: 'Now, another way of looking at acceptance or being OK with more closed states of heart is to trust that you are born with the capacity to revert back into your natural state.'

Maryam: 'Natural? Born?'

Paul: 'Yes. It's innate. I've just realised I never asked you this question: do you have children?'

Maryam: 'Yes. A daughter and a son. My daughter is seventeen and my son fifteen.'

Paul: 'Oh, how wonderful. I hope I can meet them one day. So, if you think about them when they were younger, did you ever see them get angry for longer than a few minutes?'

Maryam: 'Hmm, let me think. Well, no, not really. They could get upset quickly, but I realised that when I chose not to intervene as much as I did when I was a first-time mum, after a while they'd revert back to having fun with whatever they were doing.'

Paul: 'It's their natural state. In other words, most of the time, they don't need any help to get back there. You see, as we grow up, we acquire the uniquely human skill to *stay* upset, irritated or sad for longer periods of time – for hours or even days.'

Maryam: 'Or years.'

Paul, laughing: 'Yes, that can happen too. We have *learned* to repeat the thoughts that cause us trouble, even when the events that caused them are long gone, thereby recreating the "reality" we'd like to change over and over. As adults, we are capable of living in our minds, not in reality. The feelings that these thoughts create make them appear so real that they become truths.'

Maryam: 'What do you mean by "truths"?'

Paul: 'Well, your thoughts either manifest in actions and results through the circle of energy, ie the things you worry about actually happen, or physically manifest in your body as an infection or illness. Because our minds and bodies are one, our minds can both heal the body and make it sick. While this relationship is still broadly ignored in medicine, we can now explain and prove its mechanics scientifically. You see, there is nothing wrong at all with being sad when something sad happens. It's part of being alive. Expressing our feelings is important. For example, it can activate special capacities of our bodies or help us connect with one another. Normally our feelings serve a purpose. And normally feelings come and go. However, we can get into trouble when our more negative feelings are out of step with what's actually happening outside. Then our bodies can get sick, because of the permanent chemical reaction our minds are recreating.'

Maryam: 'So being healthy in our minds doesn't necessarily mean feeling happy all the time, right? It means that we allow our feelings to fluctuate, like children do.'

Paul: 'Well, as adults we have learned to better control some of our instinctive reactions, such as anger, fear and cravings. And that's important and helpful, too.'

Maryam: 'I'm not sure I've learned how to control cravings yet. I guess I'm still a child.'

Paul: 'I think I probably became a cook to test my willpower.'

They exchanged giggles, like two children enjoying a silly joke.

Paul: 'Now, children can simply remind us that our capacity to maintain an open state of heart, and to revert back to a more open one when it's closed, always remains available to us. Most people think of an open state of heart as a *destination*, a place we need to get to, or even convince themselves that it's something they need to acquire somehow, as if it is outside them in the first place. That makes things unnecessarily hard for them because they're looking in the wrong direction.'

Maryam: 'Where would you look?'

Paul: 'Inside – because I know it's always available for me.'

Maryam: 'You know, Paul, I've heard that many times, but to be honest, it sounds so abstract and unrealistic. I'm not really sure how to look inside.'

Paul: 'Oh, that's OK. You're not alone in that feeling. Well, here's another way of looking at it. Maybe you'll find it useful.'

Maryam: 'Sure, go ahead.'

Paul: 'I see an open state of heart a bit like a piece of cork.'

Maryam: 'Cork? Why?'

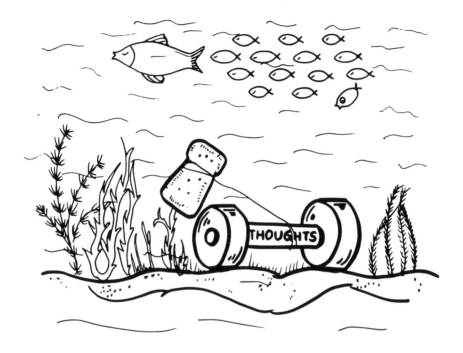

Paul: 'Cork naturally floats. When we push a piece of cork under-water and then release it, it returns to the surface. Effortlessly. When our cork is underwater – when our state of heart is closed – there's no need to push it up. It already has everything it needs inside to resurface effortlessly as soon as we release what's pulling it down – the thoughts and feelings attached to the cork.'

Maryam: 'The four domains of judgment?'

Paul: 'Yes.'

Maryam: 'I can see that. Thank you, the cork is a helpful analogy. Let me back up for a moment. We started with looking at ourselves, and how acceptance of ourselves and trust in our innate health can help us release the cork, so to speak. But what about how we look at others?'

Suspending judgment of others: the door to compassion

Paul: 'Ah yes, let's explore that together. When we met the second time in the restaurant, you wrote down a few feelings that signal to you that you are in a closed state of heart.'

Maryam: 'I did.'

Paul: 'Can you recall some of them?'

Maryam: 'Sure. I must have mentioned feeling worried, insecure, angry or upset.'

Paul: 'Now, do you believe other people experience these feelings too?'

Maryam: 'Of course they do. I guess many people feel that way – some more often than others.'

Paul: 'So, would you agree it's safe to assume we have all experienced emotions of this nature?'

Maryam: 'Yes.'

Paul: 'Now, can you see any possible value in being in these states?'

Maryam: 'I'm not sure I understand what you mean.'

Paul: 'Well, for example, what would be different in your life if you never felt angry, worried or upset?'

Maryam reflected for a moment. 'I would probably feel peaceful... yet at the same time I might not realise I am at peace because I've never experienced the opposite.'

Paul: 'That's an interesting observation. And how would you look at others who feel angry, upset, worried or irritated?'

Maryam: 'Hmmm, probably their feelings wouldn't make any sense to me. I wouldn't be able to relate to them so much.'

Paul: 'I think so, too. Although we don't like being in closed states of heart, they can be of value too. Among other things, they allow us to feel empathy and compassion for others. An esteemed friend of mine put it this way: "A broken heart is an open heart".'[2]

Maryam: 'So, are you actually saying that being in *closed* states of heart can be a path to more *open* states of heart?'

Paul: 'Yes. No doubt we're more effective in open states of heart, and we are exploring how to be there more often. At the same time, our own experiences of the pain that comes with a closed state of heart create possibilities for our hearts to soften. And soft hearts – in my experience – open more easily than rigid ones.'

Maryam smiled. 'That makes sense. Do you have an example that comes to mind?'

'Soft hearts open more easily than rigid ones.'

Paul let his mind wander for a moment. 'Have you, like me, ever had a bus, train or flight cancelled when you were trying to get home, and then got all upset, maybe even a bit condescending, with the staff because they weren't able to get the issue resolved right away due to all the confusion?'

---

2   Azim Khamisa and Jillian Quinn, *The Secrets of the Bulletproof Spirit: How to bounce back from life's hardest hits.*

Maryam, rolling her eyes and smiling: 'I have absolutely no idea what you are talking about...'

Paul: 'Thank you for your honesty. Now, I'm aware this might look like somewhat of a mundane example, yet I feel that if we can practise noticing our state of heart in everyday situations, then we can strengthen our muscles to handle the more difficult situations in work and in life.'

Maryam: 'Yes, I'm with you. Keep going.'

Paul: 'Next time you're observing the behaviour of a fellow human being in a similarly frustrating situation, instead of saying "How dare she?" you might be able to suspend your judgment and say to yourself, "Yep, been there, thought that, felt that, done that too".'

Maryam: 'We've all had one of those days, haven't we?'

Paul: 'I guess so. Now, thinking that is not the same as approving of the behaviour; it's choosing to look at it from a mindset of empathy. Thinking this way might help you keep your heart open a little longer.'

Maryam: 'That resonates with me. Knowing myself when I'm in a closed state of heart, I might also be more patient with others who are in a closed state of heart, who won't have the ears to hear whatever I feel like saying, even if it seems rational to me.'

Paul: 'Yes. Their brain tends to jump out the window, too. Isn't that what you said?'

Maryam, smiling: 'Yes.'

Paul: 'So, empathy is the first step, and your own life experience can be your empathy reservoir. Empathy is a powerful energy that has the capacity to re-open your heart, or keep it open.'

Maryam: 'And if my heart remains open then my capacity to influence the person or situation in a positive way is much higher, I guess.'

Paul: 'When the other person can sense that you are peaceful, they feel no threat coming from you. Imagine you were feeling anger instead of peace... that would probably aggravate the situation.'

Maryam: 'Oh yeah, I can confirm that one.'

Paul: 'Now, once you feel empathy, you're ready for compassion – its bigger brother. If you can empathise with someone else's closed state of heart, like a feeling of anger, because you know it yourself, you might be more able in the moment to look *beyond* their behaviours and keep perspective.'

Maryam: 'What exactly do you mean by looking beyond their behaviour?'

Paul: 'Well, if you look at the situation as a circle of energy in action, what else could you see, other than behaviour?'

Maryam: 'I guess, the feeling that caused their behaviour.'

Paul listened and looked at Maryam.

Maryam: 'OK, let's go back to the example of someone being upset with the airline staff and threatening them. They're going to file a complaint and call their manager.'

Paul: 'If we look at the behaviour of that person, we'll probably shake our heads and disapprove of his actions, unless we're upset too.'

Both giggled a bit and smiled at each other. They loved being silly together. Then Paul continued.

'Now, if we can see the feeling *causing* the behaviour, would you say we are more likely to access our capacity to suspend our judgment for a little longer?'

Maryam: 'Certainly.'

Paul: 'Why do you think that is?'

Maryam: 'Because we can see their pain.'

Paul: 'And what would that do for you?'

Maryam: 'I might feel empathy. My state of heart would open up a bit.' She paused and looked at a point in the distance until her next thought occurred. 'Once that happens, I might even be able to look beyond their feelings and recognise that there must be thoughts that created their closed state of heart.'

Paul: 'Like what?'

Maryam: 'Like worrying about implications at work or at home. I might be able to see that it's actually these fearful thoughts that have awoken the behaviour I disapprove of.'

Paul: 'Now you can see their innocence. You can see they're suffering somehow. Ironically, when others are angry, what they truly need is our compassion, not our judgment, because they're suffering. However, what we give when we're in autopilot mode is a reaction to their anger – our retaliation, which is triggered by our own insecurities when we're feeling attacked in some way.'

'Ironically, when we're angry, we need others' compassion and not their judgment, because we're suffering.'

Maryam: 'And so on – it's a circle.' She thought more about their conversation and imagined the situation with the upset traveller again. 'And still my mind goes, "Hey, is it really too much to ask that they act a bit more kindly?"'

Paul: 'You're right. If, right now, they could think differently, they would. If, right now, they could feel differently, they would. If, right now, they could act differently, they would. Right now, they don't. Because, right now, this is all they can see and feel.'

Maryam: 'Hmmm, that makes sense. So, looking at others with empathy doesn't imply I'm condoning their actions, but it helps me to stay in an open state of heart, regardless of their actions.'

Paul: 'Yes.'

Maryam: 'In a sense, practising to see innocence, as you called it, is something I do for myself, not for them, right?'

Paul: 'Yes, in the first place. And then you might wonder how you can be an effective CEO when your state of heart is closed. How can you help others be in a more open state of heart when your own is closed? You see, I like to think people always do what makes sense to them. It is either logical or psychological in their current state. So, our judgment is irrelevant – our state of heart isn't.'

Maryam: 'I hadn't looked at it that way at all. Usually when my husband is angry, especially about something that relates to me, my autopilot makes me angry as well in reaction to my judgment of his anger. And the surest way my husband can contribute to me getting even more upset is to tell me *not* to be upset, thus making a *judgment* about my feelings. And so on.'

Paul: 'I can see that. That's your judgment autopilot in action. Have you ever tried to talk your children out of their fear of something by saying, "You don't need to be afraid"?'

Maryam: 'Yes. That doesn't seem to work.'

Paul: 'Judging negative emotions or rejecting them tends to make them stronger, because for the person experiencing them, they are a physical reality. The adrenaline is already in the body, or as I like to say, the salt is already in the soup. Not seeing the feeling is not seeing the person. Rejecting the feeling is rejecting the person.'

Maryam: 'Like rejecting the rain.'

Paul: 'Yes, exactly. For feelings to change, in ourselves or in others, we need to first *accept* them. Strangely, change starts with acceptance.'

Maryam: 'So practically, I might start by saying, "I gather you're upset." That's quite different from saying, "Why are you so upset?" implying, "You shouldn't be", right?'

Paul: 'If you truly *feel* empathy, then both your presence and your words will be more likely to convey that feeling and increase the possibility of the other person's heart opening, because they will feel safer. You see, you can only judge other people if you feel superior to them.'

'Strangely, change starts with acceptance.'

Maryam: 'And in my experience, others can feel that.'

Paul: 'Indeed. Your own state of heart affects the other person's state of heart more than anything else. It's more powerful than any smart rhetoric. If you want to have healthy conversations, or make the cork float, you need to be healthy yourself. Otherwise, you'll drag the cork further down with you. When your heart is open, the words you choose to use will feel different. That's been my experience.'

Maryam: 'Thank you, Paul, that's exactly what I was wondering about. Given my life as a leader is fundamentally made up of conversations, I would like us to expand on this topic a bit more. Would that be OK?'

Paul: 'Of course, Maryam. Let's follow the flow of your thoughts.'

Truth and Tone

Maryam: 'Given my life as a leader is fundamentally made up of conversations, do you mind if we pause here for a moment?'

> 'You see, you can only judge other people if you feel superior to them.'

Paul: 'Not at all. I'm enjoying our conversation.'

Maryam: 'Me too.'

'Now, let's say that I've managed to stay in an open state of heart, in spite of having a different point of view to some of my team members. At some stage, I will need to respond to the topic at hand, right? I'm wondering, what kind of mindsets guide you and your team in these conversations?'

Paul: 'Oh, that's simple – truth and tone.'

Maryam was a bit surprised by Paul's directness. It seemed he could clearly relate to her question.

Maryam: 'Tell me a little bit more about that.'

Paul: 'Sure. Let's start with truth. Within our team, we are committed to creating an environment where we can "talk truth", because doing or not doing that affects both the quality of our decisions and our states of heart.'

Maryam: 'You're committed not to lie? I mean, that's a given, isn't it? I'm not sure if I'm following you.'

Paul: 'I'm not referring to lying about facts. Even if there might be reasons for doing so, obviously, we can't tolerate that. I mean truth in the sense of sharing what we truly *think* and *feel* about a topic – assuming we are aware of it, of course. Can you think of moments when you haven't shared that?'

Maryam: 'Hmm... yes. I think the truth is... just kidding! There are plenty of moments when I've held back.'

Paul: 'OK, and in which kind of situations does that tend to happen?'

Maryam: 'Well, I believe in moments when I feel... well, concerned that my thoughts will either not be understood, or be understood but judged, or even be used against me. Assuming innocence in myself here, I think it's a kind of trade-off I'm making – truth versus pain.'

Paul: 'Indeed, you always do what makes sense to you. And, as leader, I think there can be good tactical or legal reasons for withholding some thoughts. Yet, most of the time, like in your example, anxiety is really what holds us back. It's actually the fear of the feeling we anticipate and would like to avoid if we can. You called it being "concerned".'

Maryam: 'Ahh, I'm glad to know I'm not crazy, just human. So, what's the implication for your team?'

Paul: 'If fear is the main limitation to truth, then as Chief Energy Officers, we are co-accountable for truth.'

Maryam: 'What do you mean with that?'

Paul: 'Well, imagine for a moment people couldn't experience the feeling of fear or worry. How often do you think they would speak their mind?'

Maryam: 'Hmm, all the time, I guess.'

Paul: '... And while that may not be realistic, most of the time, the mere anticipation of judgment, and the energy of worry and inadequacy that comes with it, is sufficient to let us diminish, omit, or exaggerate what we see. If we accept that, then our role as leaders is to practise speaking in ways that let people consistently experience an energy of compassion and safety through our words, our tone and our silence. This innate capacity, in return, is rooted in how we choose to look at each other. We're not judges of each other – we are supporters. Practising looking in this way is our accountability.'

'The mere anticipation of judgment, and the energy that comes with it, is sufficient to let us diminish, omit, or exaggerate what we see.'

Maryam: 'So, like any other behaviour, the feeling and behaviours associated with openness are fundamentally rooted in a mindset.'

Paul: 'That's been my experience.'

Maryam: 'Well, after all we've talked about, I'd say that the capacity to come from this mindset, of looking at each other as mutual supporters rather than judges, is probably easier to access when I am myself in an open state of heart. And that changes.'

Paul, smiling: 'I hope it does.'

Maryam: 'I'm wondering, in moments when your team is at its best, how does that supportive mindset show up? How would I notice it's there?'

Paul: 'In my experience, it starts quite practically by us genuinely appreciating what someone is sharing, especially if it's something that might not be easy to acknowledge. Then we can move on from there. It continues with us remaining curious when someone shares views that don't make sense to us. You can feel that. There might be a reflective pause. Someone might ask a question that feels empowering and helps everyone expand their thinking, like "What support would be needed?" or "What questions do we need to find an answer to in order to take a decision here?" Again, it's not so much what we say or ask, but the energy that we transport.'

Maryam: '... because it affects the state of heart, and hence the quality of the meeting.'

Paul: 'Yes, and it's more than that. It also works the other way around. You see, truth can be quite transforming. It can transform the state of heart of a team in an instant and affect its ability to think and act together. Truth is very liberating.'

Maryam: 'Paul, you know I love your thinking, but that sounds a bit lofty. Do you have an example?'

Paul: 'Let me think... When I started here, there were quite a number of changes that needed to be made. Substantial changes. For example, we needed a completely new IT infrastructure to accelerate all of our processes, have better data for decision making, reduce costs, and improve the overall customer experience. Nowadays, our customers can use an app to let us know what they'd prefer on the menu, and we plan and cook accordingly. They can make special requests, and pay upfront via the app, so they don't have to queue at the checkout anymore.

'We had to almost completely change the menu to reflect what our customers told us they wanted, and to help us become a healthier company, which is one of the foundations of the company strategy. That meant new ways of sourcing and cooking. We also wanted to change the way we interacted with our customers and with each other, create a different spirit in the restaurant, and give everyone more space and responsibility in doing so. Then there was refurbishing the restaurant, which was long overdue, but a logistical challenge, of course. It was like open-heart surgery. And we clearly needed to get better at communicating with our customers about what we were doing.'

Maryam: 'Sounds like some really helpful, useful changes.'

Paul: 'Yes. And frightening. Many team members felt overwhelmed. But they didn't say that. Some imagined they might lose their jobs, because they didn't feel ready for what was coming, but the truth was that we needed more people, not less. They were suppressing their fear and their states of heart were closing. As a result, to deal with their discomfort, their minds were looking for rational reasons for delaying, for sticking with the status quo, or for explaining to each other why it couldn't be done. Some blamed the management for not supporting them enough or customers for being spoiled. They were even looking at ways to interpret the facts, like our ever-declining footfall, to make them look normal. Things of this nature. There was just no energy to make it happen.'

Maryam: 'I recognise that. It's the classical resistance to change.'

Paul: 'Yes, probably. The question is, where does it come from? I didn't see it as clearly back then as I do now. Everything changed one day when Joseph spoke up during our team meeting. You know, the guy who cooked Moroccan cuisine the other week?'

Maryam: 'Yup. What did he say?'

Paul: 'He said, "I was lying in my bed last night, and wondering what's going to happen to me. I mean, all the things we're proposing, in principle, they make sense, don't they? So, I was asking myself what's getting in the way for me? I eventually realised that I feel overwhelmed. The truth, is I've never had to deal with so much change at once, let alone manage it. I don't really know how to do it. I'm afraid to fail and look stupid. If I had done something similar before, I would have more courage to do it again, but I haven't. So that's how I feel."'

Paul paused for a moment and took a few deep breaths.

Paul: 'There was silence in the room. People looked at each other, then at me, then at him. And then Roberta, who's in charge of our warehouse and accounting, said, "Thank you, Joseph, for being so open and vulnerable about how you feel. It's exactly how I feel." And then others chipped in.

'The atmosphere instantly changed from one of resistance to one of empathy and understanding. The state of heart of everyone in the room changed. You can imagine the impact this had on the quality of conversations. The focus changed from resistance to figuring out ways to make it work, to supporting one another, to asking what a first step would look like, evaluating what we had to learn, and what we could build on. It felt like magic.'

Maryam: 'Joseph was sharing the truth about his feelings, and by doing so he became a catalyst for change.'

Paul: 'Yes. That's exactly what happened. He was vulnerable. And in a sense, that's a higher truth. He allowed his *humanity* to show, and that in turn allowed others to do the same. Later we spoke about this moment, and what we could learn from it for the future. Someone built on an old proverb and came up with a mantra for our team "Before talking, taste your feelings and taste your words".'

Maryam: 'Your feelings tell you something about what's going on in your heart and mind – the truth. And the taste of your words, your tone, impacts your capacity to share it.'

Paul: 'Indeed. When we put something in our mouth that's gone bad, that's foul, we'll spit it out – we empty our mouth. It's a reflex that protects us. With a bit of practice, we can do the same with our minds before we speak: We can self-empty ourselves. When we notice that our thoughts taste judgmental, defensive, or self-righteous, we can wait for a breath or longer for fresh thoughts to occur. When our words feel compassionate or inspired, we're more likely to serve fresh words to the people we work with. Words that nurture humanity.'

Maryam added a thought to her notebook.

Maryam: 'You know, Paul, it makes me smile to hear how you relate so many things to food and cooking.'

Paul: 'Well, it's a bit of fun, of course. And then, if you think about it, our words transport energy, just like food does. That's all words are – energy transported by audio waves when we speak, transported first as electrons and then as light waves when expressed in an email and read on a screen. And some types of energy open hearts, while others close them. Some words create energy, some reduce it. And as a CEO, our job is to maximise the high-frequency energy available to our part of the organisation, and channel it in the right direction. It's as simple as that. Not easy, of course, but simple.'

> 'When we put something in our mouth that's gone bad, that's foul, we'll spit it out - we empty our mouth. It's a reflex that protects us. With a bit of practice, we can do the same with our minds before we speak: We can self-empty ourselves.'

Paul opened the bag he had brought with him. 'I've brought us some tea and a few of the cookies that Anna, our Italian chef, made this week. She is a goddess and I'm pretty sure you'll find that her cookies are nothing short of divine.'

Maryam: 'Well, thank God there are leftovers.'

Paul looked at his watch. 'Shall we benefit from this wonderful view and enjoy them here before we make our way back?'

> 'Words transport energy just like food does. Some words create energy, some reduce it.'

Maryam: 'That sounds like a perfect plan.'

Suspending judgment of ideas: the door to dialogue and curiosity

As they sat on the bank, Paul poured tea into the cups he had brought from the restaurant. They sat quietly. At one point, they both took a bite of the delicious cookies and nodded in approval. They looked at each other, rolling their eyes and blinking as if to say 'Yummy' and 'You know, I'm grateful for this moment with you' and 'Thank you for your presence'. It was a happy moment.

Maryam: 'We spoke about the role judgment plays in how we're looking at both ourselves and others. You mentioned two other dimensions on our way here – ideas and life situations. Can we talk about these two as well?'

Paul: 'Oh, of course we can. In truth, these dimensions are linked to one another; we just talk about them separately. And I'm sure we'll refer back to them in our future conversations. Things of this nature don't tend to have endings... unlike the cookies we've just finished.'

Maryam: 'Well, now I know who holds the recipe for these cookies, my only obstacle to limitless indulgence is my health, I guess.'

Smiling, Paul took another sip of his tea while overlooking the meadows in front of them and waited for a new thought to enter the conversation.

Paul: 'Have a look at the wonderful red flowers on the meadow. Aren't they beautiful?'

Maryam: 'Yes, magnificent.'

Paul: 'What do you see?'

Maryam: 'Most of them, those spread over the meadows, are red tulips. I can see some early buds of roses.'

Paul: 'What other red flowers do you see?'

Maryam: 'Oh, you're right, there are some pansies, I think. Over there, closer to the edges.'

Paul: 'The scenery in front of us appears to be pretty red, doesn't it?'

Maryam: 'Yes indeed. To be frank, I hadn't even noticed before that there were so many red flowers. They seem to be everywhere now that you've pointed them out to me.'

Paul: 'Yeah, I didn't notice them before either. And if someone asked you a week from now to recall the main colour of the meadows, what would you say?'

Maryam: 'Probably, I'd say red, mostly red'

Paul: 'Now, take a moment to look at all the green out there.'

Maryam: 'There's the grass, of course, the leaves...' She scanned the scenery. 'I am now starting to see so many different shades of green, from the light – the fresh green of some of the flowers – to the darker tones in the trees. The meadow has a whole palette of different types of green. I couldn't even describe them all.'

Paul: 'There's green everywhere, right? Now, what has happened to the red?'

Maryam: 'Hmmm, it's almost gone. I mean, it's there, of course, but for a tiny moment it wasn't – how should I say it? – on my mind.'

Paul: 'So, you see different things depending on what you pay attention to.'

Maryam: 'Yes, I know, that's called selective perception.'

Paul: 'Indeed. You, well... your brain is always selecting things. It has to, because there's just too much out there. Looking at the world around us is a bit like drinking from a firehose. And there's an even more intriguing aspect I think, in how you've described your experience.'

Maryam: 'And what is that?'

Paul: 'You said that for a tiny moment, the red wasn't on your mind.'

Maryam: 'Yes, that's true.'

Paul: 'So, in order for you to actually *see* things, in this case the green, you had to literally give up seeing the red for a moment – you had to suspend it. You can't see red through a green lens.'

Maryam: 'But then it looks like we're half blind?'

Paul: 'Let me ask you a question, if you don't mind.'

Maryam: 'You know the answer.'

Paul: 'Have you ever noticed how during a normal day, as things happen – a meeting is delayed, a train has been cancelled, it rains, it doesn't rain, someone approves a budget, and someone else doesn't, a candidate accepts or declines an offer, someone presents a new idea... have you ever noticed your mind is going, "Ahh, that's nice", "Oh, that's sad", "Hmm, that's right", "No, that's wrong", "Yeah, I like that", or "I don't like that at all"?'

Maryam: 'Oh, for sure.'

Paul: 'How often would you say your mind is doing that?'

Maryam: 'Hmmm, thinking about it, I'd say quite regularly. OK, almost constantly. You make it look as if I have self-conversations all the time.' Maryam was smiling at Paul, and at herself.

Paul: 'Yes, you could say that. So do I, and that's fine. And this human chatter has a unique feature: it sorts events and ideas into one of two categories – one is desirable, the other not. One is acceptable, the other not. One will make you successful, the other will not; one will make you happy, the other unhappy. One is up, the other is down.'

Maryam: 'It's right or wrong. Beautiful or ugly. Better or worse...'

Paul: 'We're looking through *dualistic* lenses. It's one of our most pervasive thought habits that shapes how we see life. If you believe the world is split in two, so to speak, and you're not aware it's you who's doing this, that's what you will see. It will be true.'

Maryam: 'That's interesting. I hadn't noticed that or given it any particular attention.'

Paul: 'That's nothing to worry about. Our thought habits have a hard time observing themselves. Like our bodies, they need a mirror.'

Maryam couldn't help but smile, imagining her thoughts watching themselves in her bedroom mirror.

Paul: 'It's a habit we've practised since the day we were born.'

Maryam: 'What do you mean by practised?'

Paul: 'Would you agree that at any moment, since you were born, you've been trying to make sense of things?'

Maryam: 'Yes, for sure. We need to make sense of things to make choices.'

Paul: 'I think so too. And as we made these choices, some gave us what we want and made us feel loved and accepted. Others didn't give us what we were hoping for and we experienced pain in some form or another. When that happens often, we develop a pattern.'

Maryam: 'That's called learning. It helps us navigate life.'

Paul: 'Indeed. On top of that, the people who influence us, starting with our parents, add some beliefs to that. Full of best intentions, our families, friends and society tell us how to get what we want, and avoid losing what we have or getting what we don't want.'

Maryam: 'Yeah, I can see that happing. I do it with my kids to pass on what I've learned.'

Paul: 'So over time, as we continue labelling experiences and beliefs, we split our lives in half. We reject one half of life, and can get attached to the other half. With that dualistic pair of glasses, we separate what is connected, and divide what is whole. Our filters make us judges rather than explorers.'

Maryam: 'Yeah, you're right.'

Paul: 'Maybe.'

Maryam shook her head. 'Oh... dualistic thinking at work, right?'

Paul smiled. 'You see, there's nothing innately wrong with our dualistic thinking habit – as long as we can become more aware of it. It helps us make choices and decisions, which requires separation. To a degree, it also makes us see better. We tend to recognise and appreciate joy more when we've experienced sadness. We can be more compassionate when we've suffered ourselves. We see beauty compared to ugliness. We recognise the power of forgiveness when we've experienced the power of resentment. For us to see anything, we seem to need a reference point, a contrast. But then, we often believe we need to choose between the poles. The poles become reality.'

Maryam: 'I see. It's like at some stage in our lives, we pick up a pair of sunglasses that accentuate green or red, or other colours, and we end up finding them to be comfortable and a perfect fit. And while sunglasses are pretty helpful tools, after a while, we can forget that we're actually wearing them.'

Paul: 'I like your analogy. Our life-sunglasses are beliefs rooted in past experiences, education, roles, and knowledge. There's nothing wrong with wearing those sunglasses. We just sometimes forget that we're wearing them.'

Maryam: 'OK, so how do I learn to look at things from a more non-dualistic point of view, given I have my sunglasses on?'

Paul: 'Oh, there's not much you have to learn. Have you ever been in a conversation, saying to yourself, "One of us is wrong here, and it's certainly not me"?'

Maryam: 'Ah, yes. Been there, done that.'

Paul: 'And have you ever at a later stage realised that you were both partly right and both partly wrong?'

Maryam: 'Yes, I must admit that has happened more than once.'

Paul: 'And did you then continue the conversation with that awareness, and a new – a third – path appeared as a result? Not a compromise, which is still rooted in dualistic thinking, but something that neither of you were able to see before?'

Maryam: 'Oh yes, that happens.'

Paul: 'Well, I would say that in those moments, you've stepped into your innate capacity to come from a more non-dualistic stance.'

Maryam: 'So, coming from a non-dualistic stance doesn't mean that I'm agnostic on every subject, right?'

Paul: 'No, it doesn't. I personally find it relatively hard not to have a point of view. For each of us to look with a non-dualistic stance, it is helpful to simply start by noticing our dualistic mindset when it kicks in. And with awareness...'

Maryam: '...comes choice. Alright, so what can I practically look out for? How does it show up?'

Paul: 'Well, you might look at the language you're using. When you use words like "we should" or "we shouldn't", "we must" or "we mustn't", "they have to", they're likely to come from your dualistic mindset. You might be using more absolute language like "always", "never", "only", "but", "best", creating contrast, omitting or exaggerating situations.'

Maryam: 'Oh, I hear myself using those words every day.'

Paul: 'You might also notice feelings that come with your dualistic thoughts. You might feel more intense about your point of view. There might be feelings of limitation rather than abundance, more worry than hope, more knowing than wonder, more regret than acceptance.'

Maryam: 'OK. And let's say I've noticed it. What do I do then?'

Paul: 'Nothing.'

Maryam: 'Nothing?'

Paul: 'Our dualistic thoughts are just that – thoughts. When I notice them, I might be able to entertain two seemingly opposite views or ideas for a little longer and resist my initial urge to resolve them, silently wishing a choice would give me clarity and comfort.[3] Our dualistic mind doesn't like this pain of ambiguity. When we embrace the discomfort that comes from not having clarity, we might see new things, or we might not this time. Yet we can rest assured that clarity comes from confusion. Competence requires incompetence. And at times, the greatest obstacle to knowing is knowledge. These are not opposites; they are more like electric poles enabling energy to flow. They don't complement each other, they are interdependent.'

Maryam: 'OK, I think I can see that. But why are you saying knowledge is an obstacle? How can it be a problem?'

Paul: 'It's not. It's wonderful, and it's necessary to get our jobs done. Our past experiences bring knowledge and, of course, more experience. We can avoid mistakes we've made in the past – it's called learning. My team and I couldn't run our restaurant without tons of experience. But at the same time, our experience and competence come at a price.'

Maryam: 'What's the price?'

Paul: 'It can make us blind to possibilities.'

Maryam: 'And why's that?'

Paul: 'Because you will always look at what's in front of you through the lens of what you "know" from past experience. New knowledge can only arise from a lack of it. So, for us to grow, we need to embrace

---

3   This though was inspired by Roger L. Martin's wonderful article, 'How Successful Leaders Think', *Harvard Business Review* 2007

the pain of incompetence. Let me give you an example from my team.'

Maryam: 'That would be helpful, thank you.'

> 'New knowledge can only arise from a lack of it. So, for us to grow, we need to embrace the pain of incompetence.'

Paul: 'We wanted to shorten the waiting time for our customers. Actually, we wanted to shorten the entire process, from choosing a meal to collecting it, and then of course paying for it. It was clear the processing time was one of the main things discouraging people from coming to eat at our place. They'd rather grab a sandwich from one of the shops next door, not because they *enjoyed* it, but because it was *quick*. At the same time, we were committed to "celebrating and nurturing the joy of life through great food and togetherness". I shared with you when we first met how this is truly at the centre of what we love about our work.'

Maryam: 'Yes, I remember that very clearly.'

Paul: 'Now, our dilemma was this. Some team members argued that to increase the speed, we'd have to compromise on quality. We'd either need to pre-cook more things, which would negatively impact on both taste and nutrition, or offer more takeaways ourselves, like ready-made salads or sandwiches that people could take out of a fridge. Needless to say, that wasn't an expression of our purpose.

'Other team members argued that we'd not be able to live our purpose at all if we had no customers. They felt that if fast food was what people wanted, we'd have to follow their preferences. The whole idea of coming to our restaurant, choosing what was on offer – and maybe some customers wouldn't find anything they liked, standing in line to get it, then standing in line to pay for it all seemed to be obstacles preventing people from actually coming. We also faced, and are still facing, competition from high-quality delivery services. We could try to compete on price, but that would not be a winning strategy in the long run and would prevent us from doing what we really love to do.'

Maryam: 'I see the dilemma you were in. Did you try to find a compromise?'

Paul: 'Compromise was our first attempt, but that was still in essence dualistic thinking. We could have done a bit of it all – a bit of takeaway, a bit of price dropping, a bit of what we love doing, you see? So, we kept all ideas in the air. And during one conversation, we started thinking how we could help people enjoy life through great food and togetherness at work in a convenient and efficient way. That was our new challenge.

'We didn't immediately come up with a solution. The team kept asking "What if...?" or "How could we, in spite of...?" or "If we had a solution that would enable people to do this, what would it do?" I have no doubt that it was this inner mindset that eventually led us to the first stepping stones of what became a foundation of our success.'

Maryam: 'You mean the M-joy app?'

Paul: 'Yes, M-joy was born from this dilemma. Nowadays 90% of our customers use the app. It shows people the daily and weekly menus, so they can make plans to come to the restaurant. But the best bit is that they can pre-order their meal on a specific day. That doesn't just allow us to plan better and create less waste, but also people can be sure their meal or sandwich will be ready once they have ordered it.

'In the next phase, we're even thinking about putting a label on each order with the customer's name on it. People order and pay straight from the app. As a result, there is no checkout anymore. Instead of speeding up the process, we've simply skipped an entire step. When people come to the restaurant, they already know what they've ordered and go straight to the counter that serves that particular meal. We've rearranged the counters accordingly. That saves a lot of time.

'In addition, we are doing brief polls showing new dishes we're thinking of adding and asking our customers to rate them between "Wow, that would be amazing" and "Hmm, I'm not so sure". They can also make suggestions in the "I would looooove that" section, and so on. This really helps us fulfil our purpose. It's been a real game changer.'

Maryam: 'I can see that.'

Paul: 'Now, we would not have got here if we hadn't noticed our dualistic thinking urging us to take sides or find compromises between our choices. We would not have started seeing what is now apparent to us.'

Maryam: 'You suspended judgment to make better judgments.'

Paul: 'We tried, at least. It's a mindset to practise more than a thing to do. As we continued our conversations, we realised that as helpful and as necessary as experience is to do our jobs well, we tend to see – we judge – a lot of what's in front of us through the lens of what we know. As you said, it's like

'Not only are we partially blind, we can be blind to our blindness.'

wearing a pair of yellow sunglasses while looking at the meadow right now. The yellow filter will probably brighten up the environment, but it will also make it harder to see green and red and fully appreciate what the meadow has to offer.'

Maryam: 'So, as we develop expertise in a field, we can become partially blind?'

Paul: 'Yes, for sure. Yet more importantly, we can be blind to our blindness.'

Paul: 'It seems to me that we recognise sunglasses easily on other people's noses, and we like to make them aware of their tainted lenses. Yet, it's much harder to realise our own lenses and the blind spots that come with it.'

Maryam: 'So, what helped you become more mindful of the glasses your team is wearing?'

Paul: 'Well, first of all, there's nothing wrong with us having different filters – they can sharpen our view as well. The question is whether we can acknowledge their existence, and then appreciate both their virtues and limitations. In my team, we started sharing some of the moments when we realised that our sunglasses had made us partially blind or caused us to miss something. This ended up being hilarious – we heard so many funny stories. As a result, we were able to see humanity in each other. By sharing these stories, we found it easier to acknowledge that we are probably all partly right and partly wrong.'

Maryam: 'And that we're all partly blind!'

Paul: 'Indeed. We then shared with one another some of the filters and personal biases we are aware of and how they might shape our reality at times.'

Maryam: 'Oh, what did you share?'

Paul: 'I believe I shared how I often prefer trying things and then learning from experience rather than thinking things through more thoroughly and investing a lot of time into planning. I talked about how, especially when I'm in a more closed state of heart, I have a habit of labelling other people doing just that as "risk-averse", or wanting to slow down progress rather than trying to make it work. The mutual awareness we gained from sharing our humanity allowed us to remain in a curious state of mind more often, especially when sharing ideas or questions.'

Maryam remained still for a short moment and then continued. 'You've mentioned that there is a relationship between the dimensions of suspending judgment with respect to ourselves and others, and ideas. I can now see that much more. Suspending judgment in one area can help with the others.'

Paul: 'Yes. It doesn't matter where you start, it's always the same principle, the same mindset, at work.'

Maryam: 'So, what else has helped you?'

Paul: 'My team and I started asking different questions to shape what we see. Questions are a bit like sunglasses too.'

Maryam: 'Yes, I can see that. In my experience, they impact on the focus of our attention. So, what are some of the questions that guided you?'

Paul: 'We started more often with our dream rather than the problem as we could see it. We were asking ourselves, "What would a team with our dream do?" We also looked at new ideas from a curious stance, wondering, "If we were to assume this is an award-winning idea, how would we look at it differently?" Looking that way helped us see possibilities and the gold nugget hidden somewhere in an early idea. You see, we realised all new ideas on this earth have one thing in common.'

Maryam: 'And what is that?'

Paul: 'They are not perfect – *yet*.'

Maryam: 'Ha, indeed. And the obstacles can make us blind to the potential they carry.'

Paul: 'Yes, that can happen.'

Maryam: 'So, what other questions helped you?'

Paul hesitated. He was wondering if sharing more questions with Maryam would be truly helpful for her.

Paul: 'The truth is that all the questions emerged from the situation, and might never be asked that same way again. So, I can share a few merely to illustrate the mindset in action, if you like, OK?'

Maryam: 'Yes, thank you. Whatever works.'

Paul: 'Some of the guiding questions that have helped us to tap even more often into our growth mindset and embrace the discomfort that comes with feeling somewhat incompetent and not fully in control are "What would we need to learn that we don't fully understand yet?", "Where do we feel certain?" and "What might we be missing here because of our certainty?". We've started using a more appreciative lens in the way we look at others and ourselves. For example, we ask, "Who has successfully overcome a similar challenge in the past? What can we learn from that?" Or we wonder, "What are the strengths we already have that we could be using more often here?" Questions like these gave birth to some of the ideas you now see in our restaurant.'

'Ironically it's often when we need most perspective that we look at business situations from a closed state of heart, where we have least perspective.'

Maryam took notes of all these questions. Then she paused, reflected and looked back at Paul.

Maryam: 'I guess it's less about the questions themselves, more about the spirit and mindset they're coming from, right?'

Paul: 'You're spot on. They are all coming from a place of goodwill and that has helped us stay in an open state of heart for longer.

You see, ironically, it's often when we need *most* perspective that we look at business situations from a closed state of heart, where we have least perspective. We do that by judging, coercing, pressuring, hoping it will get us what we want, when all it does is make us blind.'

Maryam: 'Hmm, that's ironic indeed.'

Paul: 'Like any new idea, M-joy started out as a thought, and believe me, it wasn't a perfect one. We faced plenty of obstacles and asked many open questions along the way...'

Maryam: 'Like who'd pay for the design, implementation, operation and maintenance, I guess? And who would support each of these phases? Who on your team would be able to update the content on a daily basis? And then there are legal questions as well...'

Paul: 'Looks like we would have hit our goals much faster if I had met you back then.'

Maryam: 'Well, that's the kind of cooking I'm good at.'

Paul: 'We're looking into a new release at the moment to integrate both the feedback from our polls and a better payment system. I'd be grateful if you could have a glance at it and offer your views. We are quite good at this, but we could be missing something.'

Maryam: 'Oh, Paul, that would be a pleasure, and the least I can do to say thank you for our conversations.'

Paul: 'Thank you, Maryam. Now, what do you think? Should we start making our way back?'

Maryam: 'Yes, I guess it's time. Let's walk and talk.'

Maryam grabbed the empty cookie bag and looked at the meadow, thinking that she'd never see it in the same way again – it would now be connected to today's conversation with Paul. Then they walked shoulder to shoulder for a moment, enjoying the walk itself and each other's company.

Listening

Maryam: 'Paul, listening to you, I sense that what has helped your team be at their best is not only the mindsets you've shared with me, in particular the non-judgmental judgment, it's also how you listen to one another.'

Paul: 'Ah, thanks for highlighting that. Indeed, how we listen to each other, our customers and advisors remains a great part of our success. Yet for me, this comes down to mindsets, too.'

Maryam: 'And why's that?'

Paul: 'Because listening happens inside our minds – it's an *inside* job.'

Maryam: 'But don't you have to pay attention to others? They are *outside*.'

Paul: 'Well, let's see. Have you ever received any advice on active listening?'

Maryam: 'Yes.'

Paul: 'OK, so what kind of advice did you get?'

Maryam: 'Don't interrupt. Paraphrase what the other person said to check your understanding and signal your listening. Use your body language to show your interest. Stuff like that.'

Paul: 'Now, I'm not saying that isn't good advice, but could you do all these things and still not listen at all?'

Maryam: 'Hmm... I guess that's perfectly possible.'

Paul: 'We're *always* listening. We cannot *not* listen. The question is, what are we listening for?'

Maryam: 'So how would you describe what you and your team are listening for, then?'

Paul: 'It depends on our state of heart, which impacts on our state of mind. In more closed sates of heart, we'll be more inclined to listen to our *own* thoughts, since they give us safety. When we are in open states of heart, we are more capable of listening to be *influenced* and looking for things that we don't know, for things that puzzle us.'

Mary: 'Hmmm... I didn't really see listening as a function of our state of heart.'

Paul: 'I'd say that all our mindsets and attitudes are functions of our state of heart. We have an innate capacity to listen. Yet, for instance, we don't listen well when we experience fear. So, as a

CEO, I know that it's the feeling in the team I need to address when there's little listening going on. It's not a lack of "listening skills".'

Maryam: 'That makes sense.'

Paul: 'Your listening stance can be felt by others. If others *feel* listened to, they are more likely to be in or return to an open state of heart. When they feel you are listening with goodwill, then your listening in itself can transform worry into hope, anxiety into courage, and confusion into clarity. When teams need to cope with significant change, like in our case, listening that way is, in my experience, one of the main tools a CEO has at his or her disposal.'

Maryam: 'I've experienced what you're describing with a coach I enjoyed working with in the past. There were sessions when she hardly spoke, yet she had an unbelievable ability to make me feel heard without judgment. This helped me to reflect more freely and make new discoveries. Her mere presence affected where I went with my thoughts.'

Paul: 'I can relate to that. Listening is not the absence of talking. A dear friend of mine has this effect on me. While he does have an abundant capacity for listening without interrupting, what strikes me the most is how he seems to be listening with his heart more than with his mind. He feels things I am not clear about, or things I've tried to avoid facing. One day I asked him how he listened so well to other people.'

Maryam: 'And what did he say?'

They paused their walk and turned to each other.

Paul: 'He said he listens to people as if they're singing a song. And then he wonders what type of music it is – a gloomy blues, an angry rock, a tender jazz tune? And what would the songwriter call it – "Leave Me Alone", "Sorry, I'm Just Too Afraid", or "I'm Ready"?'

Maryam: 'Oh, what a lovely thought. That makes so much sense to me.'

They started walking again. With the sun making its way down towards the horizon and losing its strength, the temperature was dropping. Both wondered at how quickly time had passed since they had left the restaurant.

Suspending judgment of life situations

Maryam: 'Paul, you said there were four dimensions where acceptance or suspending our judgment can help us to stay in a more open state of heart and have better access to our sources of energy. We have spoken about three so far. Do we have enough time to talk about the last one?'

Paul: 'Oh yes, it's not complicated, it's just not always easy.'

Maryam: 'I'm curious.'

Paul: 'Let me ask you this. Have you ever faced, or are you maybe facing right now, decisions or situations that you can't really influence? Yet you can't ignore them either, since they impact on your work?'

Maryam reflected. 'Yes... actually quite a number of things come to mind.'

Paul: 'Like what?'

Maryam: 'Well, for example... and please keep this to yourself... I've realised that two of our execs are not getting along with each other very well, and that slows down decisions. What could be done in hours takes weeks. One of our suppliers has filed for bankruptcy. And I'm not so happy with some of my team members being spread over various time zones. What else? There's the embargo in one of our key markets. Should I keep going?'

Paul: 'No thanks, I get the picture.'

They both laughed, even though Maryam wasn't sure what was so funny. But it was a relief to laugh.

Paul: 'Now, I have no opinions on these matters, but I'm wondering, does it ever happen that you or the team get stuck in talking about these issues?'

Maryam: 'Yes, that happens. People are upset about our supplier being in trouble, it's a bummer and it took us by surprise. I hear people discussing the two executives who don't get along over lunch and in the corridor as well.'

Paul: 'What have you noticed about the impact on your and other people's energy when these thoughts fill your conversations with other people or your mind when you're on your own?'

Maryam: 'I'd say we get tense, and we can have a tendency to feel kind of powerless in the face of such obstacles.'

Paul: 'Is your heart more open or more closed?'

Maryam: 'More closed.'

Paul: 'The thoughts you pay attention to and entertain become your reality. And this reality impacts on your state of heart. Just imagine for a moment you'd fully accept the part of reality that bugs you. I don't suggest you like it, you're just accepting it for now.

How would you feel?'

Maryam: 'Hmmm... liberated. Free to move forward.'

Paul: 'You see, in a way, we all create our own heaven, and our own hell.'

Maryam: 'You mean often our pain doesn't come so much from the event itself but from the thought we're entertaining?'

Paul: 'Yes.'

Maryam: 'Well, I can see that. It's a great idea, but let's get real for a moment, OK? I can't just accept the status quo. We're here to "push the envelope", as they say, and go beyond what we see at the moment. We're here to create a better reality than the one we find. And that means I must meet my personal targets.'

Paul: 'I understand. Can I ask you another question?'

Maryam: 'Sure.'

Paul: 'If you think about the situation you've mentioned, and what you have to deal with, have you recently ever thought, felt, or said to yourself, "We can't achieve x because I am so, or he is so, or she is so..." thinking of a negative trait, or "I am not, or they are not enough"... this or that?'

Maryam thought about Paul's question. 'Yes, I think that happens quite frequently.'

Paul: 'No worries, that's also part of being human. I do the same thing. However, these two thoughts have one thing in common – they focus on *lack* or the *absence* of something. And while it might well be partly true, looking at it this way can make us blind to the abundance available in each of us and those around us. They co-author and nurture our daily drama.'

Maryam: 'So, shall I stop thinking about this or convince myself of the opposite?'

Paul: 'I'm talking about noticing and acknowledging, not dismissing, your thought. Then take it for what it is: a thought, not a truth. When you notice thoughts of something lacking, just remind yourself that the "truth" is infinitely more than your thought – truth is abundant possibility.'

Paul stopped for a moment to look for his phone, and then gave it to Maryam. 'Would you mind having a look at my phone?'

Maryam: 'Not at all.'

Paul: 'Can you describe what you see?'

Maryam: 'Well, it's black, like most phones, I guess. It's already a bit outdated, I'd say, it has a brown leather case, and some scratches on the back.'

Paul: 'How many icons can you count?'

Maryam: 'Around about twenty or so.'

Paul: 'Thanks.'

Maryam: 'Can I give it back to you?'

Paul: 'Yes. Now, can you tell me what time it is according to my phone? It's on US Eastern time, where my daughter lives.'

Maryam: 'Well, I have a sense of what time it is here, but quite frankly, I didn't pay attention.'

Paul: 'You just looked at it.'

Maryam: 'Yeah, I did.'

Paul: 'You only see what you pay attention to. In other words, attention comes *before* perception, which creates your so-called reality – the stuff that fills your mind.'

Maryam reflected for a moment on her experience. 'So, if I accept that, then I can choose to pay attention to lack or abundance. I can choose to accept what I can influence, and what I can't, so I can start seeing what is available more easily.'

Paul: 'Yes. These are some of our choices. So, if you could influence what people you lead pay attention to, what would you want them to focus on?'

Maryam: 'The possibilities. On what we can influence. On the gifts we have in our team.'

Paul: 'Can you think of a challenging situation when you have thought and reacted like this?'

Maryam: 'Yes, sometimes, when I was able to keep perspective. Yes.'

Paul: 'I'm not surprised at all. Like all the mindsets we've talked about, this one, too, is innate. When we were children and our favourite toy broke, after some tears and moaning, we got on with it and started playing with a different toy, maybe one that we had almost forgotten about. As a CEO, the question we need to ask is how can we have access to our energy more systemically, like children, especially when things are challenging?'

Maryam: 'If I look at my children, I think they have abundant access.'

Paul: 'Precisely.'

They arrived back at the restaurant just as they finished exploring this thought.

Maryam: 'I guess I have to accept that we're coming to the end of our conversation. I must admit, I didn't expect us to go this far with our feet or with our minds. It was good for both. I feel refreshed and enlivened. Our conversations always do that to me.'

Paul: 'It all started with your wonderful question about the thoughts that help us to be in open states of heart more often. Thank you for bringing it up and helping us to embark on this journey. I'm seeing new things too, and there are some thoughts from our conversation that I feel like sharing with my team.'

Maryam: 'I was wondering if I could invite you for dinner someday to meet my children and my husband.'

Paul: 'Oh, Maryam, that would be wonderful. I would feel honoured.'

Maryam: 'Great. I'll talk with my family and let you know. Have a safe trip home, Paul.'

Paul: 'Same to you. See you soon.'

Journaling

The next day it rained outside. While George was up early, Maryam decided to sleep in, and enjoy the coziness of Saturday morning a little longer than usual. She listened to the concert of the rain drops outside.

After a moment her thoughts returned to yesterday's long walk and the conversation with Paul. She felt a warm sense of gratitude for Paul's generosity and energy, for the gift of their encounters and friendship. This, she thought, is probably also a way abundance shows up in my life.

A few memories of their conversation came back, and for a brief moment Maryam thought of returning to her journal, and capturing her memories. And then, she sensed that what she really needed right now was silence, space. She felt partly confused. Then she smiled. She decided to listen to and embrace the wisdom of that feeling, trusting that clarity, her own clarity, would be born out of confusion, and that she wouldn't *need* to do something for now. It would come to her. Maryam decided that today would be her 'lazy day'. She got up, and when she arrived at the kitchen a sumptuous breakfast was waiting for her.

The next morning, before breakfast, Maryam went running to start her day. She took a long run, leading her through the park and then a small wood close to their house. It was probably after she had run half the distance, that words came to her mind. They felt clear and powerful, like bright sunlight at a beach. She didn't do anything, the thoughts were just there for her, and she could hold them all.

As she arrived home, she knew this was the moment to continue her journaling. Straight after taking her shower, she sat down, grabbed her journal, sat in her home office, and started writing, effortlessly.

1. My Power:

   - It's less the situation that creates my energy. It's my energy that co-creates the situation.

   - The use of force limits my power. Forms of force like coercion, guilt, obligation create outcomes. Yet, even if subtle and well disguised, they come at the price of a closed state of heart, limiting energy, engagement and wisdom. Ultimately, more energy will be required.

- And... no one can upset me without my permission.

2. Judgment – a special kind of thought:

   - The mere *anticipation* of judgment through others creates fear – and with it the door to insight and wisdom closes.

   - We are at our best when we can momentarily suspend our habitual judgment of ourselves, others, ideas and situations.

   - Non-judgmental judgment: we need to make judgment calls to take decisions. Our open hearts make judgment calls, our closed hearts judge.

   - Take thoughts for what they truly are: thoughts.

   - We can have strong views, lightly held.

   - Dualistic sunglasses: we're dividing our world through contrast, separation and comparison, they help us see and make us half blind at the same time.

   - There's nothing wrong with having dualistic sunglasses on. However, we throw much of life's wisdom away when we forget that we have them on.

3. Suspending judgment of self-acceptance:

   - I can trust that my state of heart will change, with or without my making.

   - Feelings naturally come and go. Being healthy doesn't mean being happy all the time, but allowing our feelings to fluctuate.

   - Rejecting unpleasant feelings is like rejecting myself.

- Strangely, the first step to shift a closed state of heart is accepting it.

- My state of heart is like a piece of cork. It gets pulled under the surface when thoughts get attached to it. When we release these thoughts, the cork comes back to the surface, on its own and effortlessly. It can't do otherwise. Like the cork, we're born with the capacity to float.

- I am always perfectly perfect with all my imperfections. So are others.

4. Suspending judgment of others – compassion:

   - A closed state of heart is our gateway to compassion: our own experiences of anger, or irritation, enable us to feel empathy for others feeling that way.

   - Our innocence: we and others always do what makes sense to us. It's either logic (for the mind) or psycho-logic (for the heart).

   - When others are in closed states of heart, experiencing anger, they need our compassion, not our judgment. They are suffering.

   - Seeing innocence in other people's actions is in a sense a 'selfish' act. It helps me to stay in an open state of heart myself.

   - Truth transforms fear. And fear is the biggest obstacle to truth.

   - Our humanity, our own truth, transforms fear almost instantly.

- Like food, words transport energy. Taste your words.

5. Suspending judgment of ideas – curiosity:

    - We grow when we embrace and lean into our 'pain of incompetence'.

    - Perceiving is like drinking from a firehose: we always select what we let in.

    - What we see is by definition always partly incomplete, partly right and partly wrong.

    - Not only are we partially blind, we are blind to our blindness.

    - Luckily we tend to have different blind spots. In an open state of heart, our respective blindness is seen as a gift.

    - We are always listening, the question is: to whom?

    - I'm probably listening, when the other feels listened to.

6. Suspending judgment of life – abundance:

    - Attention comes before perception. We only see what we pay attention to.

    - We create our own heaven and our own hell through the thoughts we entertain.

    - We have more energy and power when we focus on what we can influence, and accept what we can't.

    - Abundance is a thought, scarcity is a thought. And energy goes... where thought goes.

CHAPTER 5

Soul: Before Thought

'Yes, the mind is good at thinking. But so much so
that most humans, like Descartes, think
they are their thinking.'

Richard Rohr

'The heart has its reasons which reason knows nothing of.'

Blaise Pascal

'The conscious mind is a potent tool, but it's slow, and
can manage only a small amount of information at once.'

Steven Kotler and Jamie Wheal

'What man actually needs is not a tensionless state
but rather the striving and struggling for a worthwhile goal.'

Viktor E. Frankl

A month later, Maryam invited Paul over for Sunday lunch at her house. Paul's wife was visiting his mother-in-law with their children, and he would join them there a week later. He brought some of the cookies that Maryam had enjoyed so much when they'd sat on the bank last time, and the recipe, which put a big smile on her face.

Maryam showed Paul around her house, which was warm and full of memorabilia and pictures that celebrated special people, places and moments in her family's lives. They enjoyed a sumptuous meal cooked by Maryam and her husband, George, and it turned out that desserts were George's speciality. As they talked about their families, Paul enjoyed the hospitality, which soothed the sadness he felt from his family being away.

After lunch, George took the kids to the cinema, giving Paul and Maryam time to continue their conversation. Paul sat on the patio, enjoying the view and peacefulness of Maryam's garden. After giving George and the kids a hug, Maryam joined Paul with two mugs of coffee and the cookies he had brought.

Paul: 'It feels good to be at your place and meet your family. I feel blessed being here.'

Maryam: 'Oh, it's our pleasure, Paul.'

Paul: 'And lunch was superb. I loved the sprinkle of walnut oil in the soup, which gave it a special, fine taste. If I didn't know better, I'd ask you to join my team.'

Maryam: 'Oh, thank you for the compliment. To be honest, it was actually my husband's idea. We both enjoy cooking. He often has great ideas, yet most of the time I'm much better at executing them. Don't tell him, though.'

Paul, smiling at Maryam: 'I won't. And it sounds like you're a good team. Unfortunately, I can't hire you both.'

Maryam laughed and poured coffee into Paul's cup.

Love: the anchor

Maryam: 'I really enjoyed our last conversation overlooking the meadows.'

Paul: 'Oh, me too. I talked about some of it with my team. I'm curious to hear what you've taken away, and what reflections you've had since.'

Maryam: 'Well, I've asked myself the same question, you know? I've reflected a lot on how our ability to make judgments is a universal gift, yet also, if done in autopilot mode, a source of the very problems we're trying to solve. And that simple awareness is impacting on me. It's like a gentle yet powerful wave. Like water, the awareness surrounds me everywhere, changing my reality without me wanting to change anyone.

'I'm not explaining myself well... I can't say that the world around me has changed, but I'm looking at it differently. I've changed what I pay attention to and what I don't. I'm looking differently at myself, and more importantly, at others.'

Maryam poured some more coffee into Paul's cup, and then into hers.

Maryam: 'Somehow, I feel more peaceful. Don't get me wrong, the pressure and workload haven't changed. Yet there is – how should I say it? – more space between things happening, people doing or saying things, and my reaction to them. I feel like I'm responding more often, rather than reacting. There's more joy, too. And people around me seem to feel that.

'One team member approached me last week and told me that she felt I had changed. At first, she couldn't tell how, but it was important to her to tell me how much she had enjoyed working with me recently and that she wanted to stay on my team. That surprised me, because when I arrived, I had a sense she wasn't feeling part of the team, and I knew through the grapevine that she was looking for alternative roles. In the weeks since you and I started talking, she's been much more engaged, and she's made great progress on the projects she's in charge of. At the start, I felt I almost needed to bother her just to get updates. I guess she was looking for ways to minimise the time we spent together. This last month, she has almost been seeking me out, if you know what I mean, and wanting to discuss things with me.'

Paul: 'Have you asked her what has made her feel this way?'

Maryam: 'Yes, I did. And I was surprised how open she was about her feelings. She said that my energy and my way of thinking were bringing out the best in her. She said it felt easy to speak her mind to me. And she's right... there's more energy in me, in her, and in the team overall. The quality of our conversations has improved. We're laughing more often, just for the sake of it. And we're translating our energy into action more easily.'

Paul: 'What has changed in you? How do you feel about this?'

Maryam held her cup of coffee in her hands and glanced at the flowers and trees in her garden. She then responded.

'I think it's simple, Paul. My heart is open more often. Not all the time, it just re-opens quicker. It has... softened. That's the best way of describing it. And I don't resist it. I've become less worried that having an open heart could be a dangerous kind of place to be in.'

She paused, and Paul looked at her quietly.

Maryam: 'And my focus, the focus of my thoughts, has changed. When I first met you, I often felt frustrated. My attention went to how I felt, how others caused me to feel that way, and how they'd need to change for me and those around me to feel better and get good results. And to be honest, more or less overtly, I used all the techniques I'd learned in my "school of leadership": convincing, carrot and stick, creating feelings of obligation or guilt... those sorts of things. Doing these created results, yet I realised they were also – at the same time – the source of how I felt. And more importantly, the source of the problems I wanted to resolve in the first place. I was blind to the dimension of energy – the energy I either created or blocked.

'As I became more aware of the relationship between mindsets and the state of heart, I gently shifted my attention to how I could transform my state of heart and the states of others' hearts. And to be clear, I'm still a work in progress. Yet now I apply less force, but feel more powerful. That surprises me.'

Paul: 'And how do you feel about that?'

Maryam: 'A bit puzzled on one hand. All this doesn't fit in to what I've believed and experienced so far in terms of my leadership and leadership in general. I feel like I've lived in a room for many years – a room that I know very well by now. I know every corner of it. It is reassuring. But I have just discovered a new door in the back of that room which I've never seen before, let alone opened. It was always there, but not for me. Now I've opened it and crossed the threshold. I'm gently exploring this room, discovering my new space gradually because – it's new terrain. But it feels good. I feel better, and I'd like to discover the rest of the house.'

Paul: 'Maryam, you've touched the essence of leadership.'

Maryam: 'What do you mean?'

Paul: 'Love. That's your new room. You've become a more loving leader.'

Maryam: 'Well, Paul, I'm not sure if I want to call it love. Doesn't that take it all a bit too far?'

Paul: 'What would you call it then?'

Maryam: 'I don't know. Love's just not a word we use in business.'

Paul: 'I know. That's OK, and you don't have to. I don't call it love openly because I don't want to get raised eyebrows and rolling eyes. Many have bought into the belief – the mindset – that love is a private matter, and it should be excluded from business. And their experiences have proven them right. Then that mindset co-creates the reality they live in. This is what we have been talking about since we first met, and you seem to have changed your point of reference.'

Maryam: 'My point of reference?'

Paul: 'A CEO makes the happiness, wellbeing and growth of others – rather than her own – her main point of reference. Isn't that love? And when we talked at the meadows, we talked about how, as a CEO, we can choose to be accepting of people and life. Isn't that love? And – strangely, or maybe unsurprisingly – by doing this, we as leaders are more likely to be both fulfilled and successful. Our energy attracts and affects others. People thrive in the presence of people who come from a deep sense of humanity and bring loving kindness to all interactions, regardless of the roles of others and the specific situation. In our presence, people experience much less or almost no fear, and are then willing and more capable of going above and beyond, because they have access to their innate energy. And in its highest and purest form, that energy is love.'

Maryam sat still for a moment. 'I see. You mean love is a "come-from", right?'

Paul: 'Yes, you could say that – a "come-from", an inner stance, a feeling, a leadership choice. I believe that true leadership both comes from and nurtures the same qualities as true love: things like understanding, kindness, joy, compassion, forgiveness and humility. Such leadership comes from and creates high-vibration energy, whereas fear, guilt or anger creates low-vibration energy. The vibration is reflected in our states of heart. The closer we get to loving states, the better people we lead will work, naturally. At the same time, coming from a loving place is the only way to achieve just that.'

Paul took a sip of his coffee, savouring the smell of it. 'In my view, everything we've talked about is merely another way or mindset to transform energies associated with fear, anger or guilt into energies associated with love, hope and compassion, and then direct them towards our goals. That's really all CEOs do.'

Maryam: 'When you put it like that, I can see how our conversations are all anchored in the same intention. Why didn't you refer to it as love straight away, then?'

Paul: 'If I had, how would you have reacted?'

Maryam: 'Hmm, to be honest, I may have dismissed it. And even now, I must admit it sounds too simple to be true.'

Paul: 'That's why. You see, Maryam, I genuinely can't teach you anything. As Galileo said, "You cannot teach a man anything, you can only help him find it within himself." I can only help you see it for yourself, or accompany you on your journey. Personally, I believe that the greatest truths, the universal truths, are simple, but often they can only be felt, not explained. And because the world seems so complex, at times we buy into the belief that truth must be complex, too.'

Maryam: 'Well, I am glad we've started travelling together. I'm wondering, where we will end up today?' She and Paul chuckled.

Paul: 'You see, I believe that being a loving leader, or a CEO, is not a technique, solution or destination. Rather it's a never-ending journey of self and life discovery. It's the discovery of the new room you've talked about. It's more something you can choose to be and discover, and less something you do and apply. Love isn't something you'll preach, it's the way you'll choose to look.'

Maryam: 'I sense that. And I'm OK with that, I think. It's just that "love" doesn't seem to fit into my daily experience of business. I'm not sure I can be "loving" all the time. I mean, I'm not, let alone others I need to deal with. This all sounds a bit warm and fluffy to me.'

Paul: 'Yeah, it does. And that's because humans actually are warm and fluffy. If you think about it, there are only two drivers, two motivations for all human behaviour.'

Maryam: 'Hmm, what are they?'

Paul: 'See if this is true for you. Ultimately all humans want to feel loved and safe. They want to feel accepted and avoid feelings of emotional or physical pain. Looking at both others and myself this way makes it easier for me to see our innocence and be more forgiving with myself and others.'

Maryam reflected for a moment. She wondered if she could see her own behaviours, as well as those of her family and colleagues, as a function of the desire to be loved and safe, or avoid pain.

Maryam: 'Hmm... it's strangely simple. It makes a lot of sense to me. We spoke about this last time, didn't we? When I look at fellow humans this way, I can "look beyond" their behaviour, while not necessarily agreeing with it or liking it. I can still choose how to feel, at least after the first rush is gone.'

Paul: 'Indeed. And if you accept that energy, the true currency of any CEO, is governed by the laws of nature, and if you accept that our need to feel loved is one of these fundamental laws of nature, then you can choose to work with it or against it. It truly is your choice. Pain, or the fear of pain, closes our hearts and reduces access to our energy sources. Feelings associated with love and safety open our hearts and provide access to our energy sources. If you're trying to get energy through force or coercion, that ultimately won't get you what you want, or it will create what you want to overcome, like a lack of engagement. The price will be higher than the gain – the energy you invest to get it will be higher than the energy output, because you're literally working against nature. And nature is stronger than you.'

Consciousness: becoming the captain of our soul

Maryam: 'If you don't mind, why don't we carry on from here and explore my new room a bit more? I'm pretty sure there are parts I haven't even noticed yet. I really would love to look around and see what else is there that might help me to lead in loving ways and nurture open states of heart more often.'

Paul: 'That would be wonderful. Maybe the room has windows, and we can pull the blinds up and let in some light to see better. First, though, why don't we take stock for a moment?'

Maryam: 'Alright.'

Paul: 'In your own words, if a good friend asked you what we've been talking about, what would you say?'

Maryam folded her hands, allowing one hand to gently caress the other while she looked into the sky. It helped her mind to wander.

Maryam: 'I'd say we've looked at business through the lenses of energy, different frequencies and sources of energy. Then we've talked about how the "circle of energy", as you called it, is in a sense the doorway to our energy. Each of us, and all the people we lead, has access to more or less energy depending on our state of heart. Our state of heart, in return, influences and is impacted by our thoughts, our habitual thinking and our mindsets. In our last conversation, we looked at four mindsets that can help us to nurture and stay in open states of heart in the face of challenges, all of them relating to our capacity to suspend judgment. So, in essence, I'd say we've looked at the role of feelings and thoughts. Is that a fair way of summarising our conversations so far?'

Paul: 'Oh, Maryam, I wish I had your capacity to be so succinct at times. Yes, I think that's a beautiful summary. Indeed, mindset is the main leverage for a CEO. Our own thoughts create and change our own reality. Now, let me ask you this. We talked about behaviours, feelings and thoughts. What then comes before thought?'

Maryam: 'Before thought? I'm not sure I understand what you mean.'

Paul: 'I mean, who's aware that you are thinking?'

Maryam: 'Well, me.'

Paul: 'Precisely. So, who is "you?"'

Maryam: 'Oh, that's a big question. I guess I'm many things. I'm a manager, I'm a mother, a wife, a daughter, a colleague, a sister, a friend...'

Paul: 'I didn't know you had a sister. We all step into roles and responsibilities. They describe what we do. But can they define who we truly are? For example, when you weren't married, were you not you? And when you weren't a manager or a mother, were you not you? And isn't what you believe being a mother or daughter is changing over time?'

Maryam: 'Hmm. Well, if you look at it that way, then I'd say I am my memories – the memories of my life that come from doing all the things I've done and experiences that have probably shaped the way I think.'

Paul: 'These memories are definitely a part of you, and they surely impact on how you think. However, your memories change and are merely a partial picture you reconstruct every time you access it. Imagine for a moment you lost all your memories as the result of an accident. Would your family dump you because you are not "you" anymore?'

Maryam: 'Well, no, of course not.'

Paul: 'Why?'

Maryam: 'Hmm, because... I'm more than that. I'm much more than my memories.'

Paul: 'I believe you are infinitely more. And, it seems, we all sense that intuitively. So, if it's not your memories, who are you then?'

Maryam: 'Well, OK, I must be my brain, right? It's my brain creating and holding my memories. And as long as that's working, I'm considered alive… and vice versa.'

Paul: 'You do indeed need your brain for your body to function and navigate through life. It's an exceptionally sophisticated and powerful organ, allowing you to do wondrous things. But it's not you. We wouldn't be sitting here, enjoying each other's presence and your lunch, if that was all you were. We didn't come here for a meeting of the brains. Your brain has changed tremendously since you were five years old. You could say it's not the same brain anymore. But were you not you when you were five?'

Maryam: 'Ah, I see. You're alluding to the cells that form my body, including my brain. I am my cells.'

Paul: 'Your cells are also unlikely to be you. As a matter of fact, many of the cells sitting in front of me right now are not the same ones that would have been here a year ago. So, if we sat here a year ago, would I not have met you?'

Maryam: 'OK, let's go deeper then. Cells are made of molecules, and they're made of atoms. But then I guess they left me too when my cells renewed or died.'

Paul: 'They did. They are somewhere else now. Maybe some of them have become part of the trees in front of us. So what are your current atoms made of?'

Maryam: 'I'm not an expert in physics, but from what I recall they're made of protons, electrons and neutrons, right?'

Paul: 'You're right, and we could go deeper and discover quarks and other particles. Essentially, in laymen's terms, they are all forms of energy. And in between them is...'

Maryam: '... a lot of space.'

Paul: 'Or, if you've ever delved into quantum theory, a lot of possibility.'

Maryam: 'I had no idea you were that interested in physics.'

Paul, laughing, 'Well, I cook for a living. That's applied physics, isn't it? We nurture and transform energy – physical and emotional energy – through preparing food.'

Maryam, smiling: 'Alright, so let's go back to your question. I'm not my memories, although they are helpful. I'm not my brain, although that's a super-cool organ. I'm not my body, although that is also super-helpful and I do spend a lot of time and energy to keep it in shape. I seem to be made of many things that are not me... which is kind of weird, now that I think about it. So, who am I?'

Paul: 'I would suggest you are all these things too, just not permanently. Your thoughts, your feelings and your body are always changing. Your "true self" must be that which is permanently there. You are not your thoughts. You are not your body. You are infinitely more. You are that which is aware that you're having thoughts. I like to refer to my true self as my soul or consciousness.'

As Paul paused for a moment before continuing, Maryam reflected.

Maryam: 'Are you sure about that?'

Paul: 'No, it just makes great sense to me. And while there are many spiritual, philosophical, religious and even scientific organisations and traditions that continue exploring this most fundamental question – "Who am I?" – and of course its implications, there can by definition be no certainty. We're in the realm of faith, and faith requires uncertainty. My intellect alone won't be able to grasp it, because it is only a part of who I am. So, to answer your question, I can only know for sure once I've died; or rather, once my body has died.'

Maryam: 'Promise me we'll continue our conversation then.'

Paul looked at Maryam with a smile that reflected kindness, joy and a deep sense of humility.

Paul: 'Oh, I have little doubt we will. And we don't have to wait. I suggest we look at the implications of looking at life, including work, as if we accepted the possibility that we are our intangible selves – our souls – making tangible experiences by interacting with a seemingly material world through the thoughts, senses and feelings that our bodies enable us to have. Would that work for you?'

Maryam: 'OK. Let's give it try. I have nothing to lose, right?'

Paul: 'Let's see...'

Maryam, smiling: 'Alright, so where shall we start?'

Paul: 'How would you say you experience daily events most of the time?'

Maryam: 'First I see, hear, feel, smell or touch something.'

Paul: 'So, through your senses, right?'

Maryam: 'Yes.'

Paul: 'And once these sensations have entered your body, what allows you to experience anything at all?'

Maryam: 'Well, I guess it's essentially my thoughts, beliefs, memories, and my feelings.'

Paul: 'All these capacities help you to make sense of things, right? So, the way it looks, we exist through our thoughts, which then create feelings.'

Maryam: 'That's the circle of energy.'

Paul: 'Yes. So, "I think, therefore I am" is more or less the underpinning life assumption. And it makes sense. It's how life comes across, because my feelings and thoughts are very real to me.'

Maryam: 'Nowadays you can even observe and measure them in real time on MRI scanners.'

Paul: 'You can indeed. Thoughts and feelings are forms of energy that can be measured. Now, if you look at yourself from that perspective, how comfortable would you feel letting go of or suspending an opinion or a belief?'

Maryam: 'Very uncomfortable. My beliefs and opinions are not just thoughts that come and go; they say something about how I see myself, how I'd like to be seen, how I see the world. They reflect all I've learned so far. It's precious stuff. So, letting go of a thought or belief, even worry, would mean letting go of a part of myself. It would actually be like dying a little.'

Paul listened quietly to Maryam's reflections.

Maryam: 'We seem to have an attachment to some of our thoughts, even if they are unpleasant, right?'

Paul: 'That seems to be the case. We are *all* attached to some things and some thoughts. And there's nothing wrong with that. As you've just described it, this attachment is an integral part of our human experience. Thoughts are the very stuff that our so-called identity – what we believe to be "us" – is made of.'

Maryam: 'But then, the stronger my thoughts, my judgments, my beliefs, the more alive I would feel.'

Paul: 'And when you are alone, with nothing to do and no one to talk to, instead of embracing stillness, you might feel an urge to occupy your mind with television, problems, activities until late at night, hoping to feel alive.'

Maryam: 'And I might not even be aware that in a way, I am... unconscious.'

Paul: 'Yes, I'd say in such moments we are unconscious. We are flying on autopilot, yet have forgotten it's switched on.'

Maryam: 'Oops, sounds like a recipe for a crash-landing.'

Paul: 'Well, we're probably all more or less junior pilots collecting flight-hours. If you look at it that way, then mindfulness is the practice of reminding ourselves that we are the pilot, not the plane.'

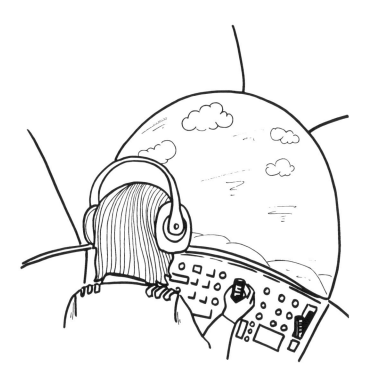

Maryam: 'So, does that mean I need to separate myself from my thoughts and feelings?'

Paul: 'I'm not sure we can or should. The plane is made up of the beliefs and mindsets we've created. It's normal we're attached to them – we've invested years into building them. But as we start seeing the plane for what it truly is – a powerful tool with some effective and some worn out parts – we can decide for which purposes we want to use it. We decide on the destination, because we are the pilot, not the plane. We can make more conscious use of the vessel. We determine which thoughts we give energy to, and which not. And, our state of heart is a key instrument on our dashboard, telling us about the state of the plane we're flying and if we're flying it safely.'

Maryam was thinking of a line in a poem[4] she had come across a few times. She hadn't been able to understand why it touched her each time she read it, but in this moment she saw a connection.

Maryam: '"I am the captain of my soul"?'

Paul: 'You are indeed.'

Maryam: 'Paul, I must admit that although you surprise me every time we meet, I didn't expect us to have a conversation about physics, soul and consciousness this afternoon. I don't have many occasions to talk about these things, so I'm truly enjoying it. At the same time, I can't help feeling a bit uncomfortable, because I can't see how this is relevant to our conversation about leadership. I mean, how do we move from the sub-atomic and soul level back to profit and loss, KPIs, customers and project meetings? You see, in my department, last time I checked, we still had bodies meeting, some with very strong thoughts, making material decisions and visible actions. I don't mean to sound condescending here; I'm just struggling to relate this soul and "true self" stuff back to the office. How can this perspective help me in any way to stay in an open state of heart more often, and be a better Chief Energy Officer?'

Paul: 'Oh, Maryam, thank you for being so honest and candid about your concerns. I fully understand your question – I've asked myself the same question again and again, and continue to do so. All we're doing here is expanding our understanding of what we call truth or reality, because we'll look at everything we experience – including work – through that lens. If we keep the same lens, we don't see more even if we look harder. But that doesn't answer your question, and I don't have an answer I can

---

4   *Invictus*, William Ernest Henley

offer straight away. Maybe it'd be better if we looked at some real-life situations, OK?'

Maryam: 'Yes, please. *I love* practical things.'

Presence: Owning your iPod

Paul: 'Maryam, can you think of situations where someone has said or done something that made you feel angry or upset, but it took you a while to find the right moment to talk with that person? Maybe you delayed the conversation because you didn't feel comfortable enough to have it.'

Maryam: 'Oh, for sure. Plenty.'

Paul: 'Me too. Now, have there been times when your irritation or annoyance over the situation has increased over the days following it?'

Maryam: 'Of course.'

Paul: 'Would you mind describing that experience? How did that show up for you?'

Maryam: 'It's constantly on my mind. I think about it when I wake up, while in the shower, during breakfast, and in the car. It comes up during meetings and breaks, when I brush my teeth, and it can even stop me from sleeping. Depending on the intensity of the situation, it may happen in some of these places or all of them. The thoughts can literally consume me.'

Paul: 'What do you tend to think about?'

Maryam: 'Well, I'm often in a way rehearsing the conversation that I imagine or hope will take place one day. I'm thinking about how

I'll justify my own actions and make it clear why what the other person did was wrong, and the impact it had on others and on me. I'm imagining the other person's reactions and my line of defence, and so on and so forth. Sometimes I talk to myself as if I was in the conversation in that moment. My husband notices that at times, and says, "Maryam, are you talking to yourself?" I usually feel a bit embarrassed when that happens, since I thought I was alone.'

Paul: 'OK, so your mind is filled with things, right? The thoughts about the situation or person are filling the space up here.'

As he was saying that, Paul pointed to his forehead with his finger and drew an invisible square on it.

Maryam: 'Yes, you could say that.'

Paul: 'Out of curiosity, when you are in that state of mind, how conscious are you about the fact that you are having these "conversations"?'

Maryam: 'Hmm, I'm not sure. I mean, I clearly remember these moments, so it's not like it's a dream or something. On the other hand, I often feel like I am in some kind of thought bubble. I can think of many instances when I've left the house in the morning without my jacket or laptop – things that I would obviously need. I even drove to the wrong airport one day, and almost had an accident on another occasion – there was stop-start traffic on the motorway, and I hadn't noticed the traffic had stopped again. When I hit the brake, I heard the horns blaring from the cars in front of and behind me; it was like I woke up. It's hard to admit, but I can't have been fully aware I was even driving.'

Paul: 'It was as if you were on autopilot, right?'

Maryam smiled, raising her eyebrows: 'Yes. I guess *someone* must have been driving the car up to that point.'

Paul: 'Alright. Now, how would you describe how you're feeling when you're on autopilot? What's your energy? What's your state of heart like?'

Maryam: 'Well, I can only say this in hindsight – I'm tense. My heart is pumping and my chest is contracting as if I were fully there, but I find it hard to focus on other things. I feel consumed. And this seems to show up on my face and how I come across to the world. Sometimes my kids or colleagues approach me and ask, "Are you alright, Maryam?" to which I tend to respond, "Yeah, I'm fine." I'd say I'm in a closed state of heart.'

Paul: 'OK. And let me ask you – when you feel intense in that way, have you ever found yourself engaging in gossip? Not necessarily in a nasty way, but giving in to the urge to share with others how bad your situation is because of someone else, secretly hoping for sympathy, or endorsing negative stories others have to share with your own personal examples, or simply by nodding, rolling your eyes, or making comments such as "Welcome to my world"?'

Maryam: 'Well, Paul, only because it's you, I'll admit to that. Sometimes, it can be a bit like a dry run of the actual conversation that hasn't yet occurred. Before it was just in my mind, but now it's verbal and I'm engaging others. I don't do that often, of course, but there are moments when it's a relief.'

Paul: 'I don't think you're alone. And... is it a relief?'

Maryam: 'Just for a moment. Then the feeling seems to get stronger. I feel I am even more right, more hurt, and more "ready" to "bring it on".'

Paul: 'Oh, Maryam, I so enjoy your honesty. It's refreshing every time we talk. Now, let's set that scenario aside for a moment. Can you think of situations where something similar happened? Again, you didn't talk with the person who triggered your feelings, but on this occasion the intensity of your feelings faded away. And then, once you met with that person, you either didn't feel a strong need to talk about what had bothered you anymore, or were able to chat with them from a calm and compassionate perspective?'

Maryam: 'Yeah – that happens too at times. Not often, though. Sometimes, after a while, I can't clearly remember what upset me in the first place. For example, I can think of times with my husband when we've argued and been pretty upset with one another. And then, after a good night's sleep, we've just looked at each other and hugged, whispering, "I'm sorry" or "It's OK, darling". We have forgiven one another, and our hearts are wide open. We know deep down inside there is nothing to talk about, because our anger doesn't actually exist anymore. And so we get on with things. In other instances, though, we keep staring angrily at one another for days.'

Paul: 'Again, I believe you could find many people with similar experiences. I can relate to all your examples. Now, in both instances, you didn't have an opportunity to talk – to solve the issue, so to speak – so what was the difference between these two experiences?'

Maryam: 'Hmm, that's a good question. For some reason, my thoughts are quite loud in the first scenario – when I feel angry for days. They are really intense with a lot of energy, like a live concert at Wembley Stadium – where I couldn't hear anything else even if I wanted to. In the other instance, my thoughts seem to quieten down like background music in a supermarket that I only really notice when I pay deliberate attention to it.'

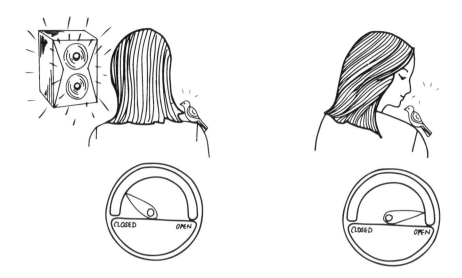

Paul: 'Oh, what a wonderful metaphor. Well, as we both know, thoughts are like music, a form of energy. They are electric impulses.'

Maryam: 'This also means that to exist, they need to be fed, or they will simply run out of steam.'

Paul: 'Indeed. The energy doesn't actually go away; it transforms – quite literally – into feelings, words, actions and physical conditions. If thoughts are frequently repeated, they create stronger connections between our synapses, or our neural pathways. Over time, they become habits, mindsets or beliefs.'

Maryam: 'So, the way we give energy to our thoughts is by giving them attention. Every time we think about them again, consciously or not; every time we talk about them, they become stronger, right?'

Paul: 'Indeed. And there's nothing wrong with that – that's how our mind works. This is how we learn new skills, but this is also how we create and influence our energy, our state of heart, and ultimately our reality.'

Maryam: 'Hmmm, it's interesting. When we met last month in the park, we looked at the content of our thinking. Now we seem to be looking at the process of our thinking and becoming observers.'

Paul: 'That's it! When you're mindful, you start observing the music in your head that you mentioned. You see, when we're in closed states of heart, we can be a bit like people with wireless headphones listening 24/7 to a playlist called "The Best of Labelling and Judgment", yet we're not even aware we're listening to pre-recorded music in the first place. If we can realise it's the music we're listening to that closes our hearts, rather than the events or people the music is about, we can consider our options. We can change the playlist, lower the volume, or even take our headphones off and realise we are not the music, but the one choosing to listen to it.'

Maryam: 'Ahh – I like that. Changing the playlist is like changing the content of our thoughts. For example, we might notice and eventually suspend our judgment by shifting from repeating negative assumptions about someone's motives to wondering what makes them feel unsafe.'

Paul: 'Yes. Now, when your state of heart happens to be closed, and the negative energy emanating from your thoughts is too strong, you might find thinking in that manner hard to do, or even impossible. And that's when it's a more realistic first step to lower the volume.'

Maryam: 'OK, that makes sense. So, lowering the volume means cutting the energy supply that feeds our thoughts, and not entertaining them anymore, right? Every time I'm attending to a thought or story again, or every time I engage in gossip hoping for a bit of relief from my pain, the thought actually becomes stronger instead of weaker.'

Paul: 'Indeed. So how could you lower the volume?'

Maryam: 'Well, I might just interrupt what I'm doing, take a walk, take some deep breaths.'

Paul: 'Yeah. Anything that helps you to interrupt your thinking pattern. You might with practice choose not to repeat the thought.'

Maryam: 'And then I could take off my headphones.'

Paul: 'Now, when you take off your headphones, you're changing your stance. You remember that you simply have a tool in your hand, albeit a powerful one. You remember that you are not your thought, just as you are not your eyesight or your hearing. All of these are miraculous tools, but your true self, your soul, is the artist using them. If you come from that place, you are the one in charge of your iPod. Otherwise it's the iPod – or your thoughts and feelings – that takes charge of your life.'

Maryam was picturing herself taking off her headphones and looking at them.

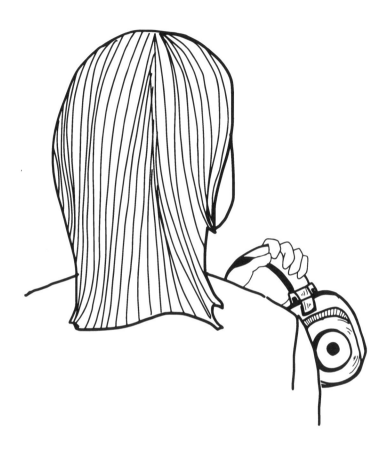

Presence: becoming an observer

Maryam: 'So, if it's our mind, our internal iPod, that affects our state of heart, then there are really two ways to open our hearts. One path is to focus on the content of our minds and nurture mindsets that help us maintain or reconnect with our open state of heart more often, regardless of life events. That's what we've been talking about since we first met, right?'

Paul: 'Yes.'

Maryam: 'The other path is changing our stance from "I am my thought" to "I am the one observing my thought".'

Paul slowly and quietly nodded. He could feel Maryam's emerging sense of joy that came from seeing more clearly something beautiful that had always been there.

Maryam: 'I was never fully aware of my mental iPod before. I'm wondering – how could I possibly not have been aware of it? And how have I become aware of it? And could I really take the headphones off? I mean, aren't we always thinking?'

Paul: 'Let me ask you a question. When you had that argument with your husband, and the next morning you chose to forgive each other and simply carry on, what had happened between the time of the argument and the moment the two of you hugged? What helped you transform a low-frequency energy into a higher-frequency energy?'

Maryam: 'I... I'm not really sure what I did, if anything. Somehow, though, I must have managed to lower the volume, and then completely switch off the angry music. In the morning, I saw him and he saw me the way we normally see each other – with loving, appreciative eyes.'

Paul: 'So, would you agree that although you hadn't consciously done anything, you already possessed the capacity to transform energy? You had no particular training, right? You hadn't read a self-help book that night? You didn't call a wise friend? You didn't take any observable action?'

Maryam: 'No, I didn't. Hmm, looking at it that way, I'd say I've done this countless times.'

Paul: 'You see, when that's happening, it's your innate wisdom at work, guiding you. This wisdom is not outside of you; you carry it with you all the time. All you and I are talking about is how we might access this innate ability more often, more consciously. And how can we nurture it so we find ourselves in lower states of heart less often in the first place?'

They sat quietly, Maryam feeling peaceful and excited at the same time. She felt there was a new dimension unfolding in front of her. She could feel it, but not describe it. And she didn't want to describe it.

Paul: 'Are you OK to try a small experience?'

Maryam: 'Sure.'

Paul: 'Have you ever done any meditation or related practices that use breathing as a foundation?'

Maryam: 'Not really. I've read about it and followed some sessions as part of a workshop, but I haven't practised it myself.'

Paul: 'Oh, that's perfectly fine. Let me ask you: have you ever observed football or rugby players right before an important penalty kick in front of millions of supporters, both in the stadium and watching on TV?'

Maryam: 'Yes.'

Paul: 'What did you notice about how they prepare? I mean, apart from praying to God or imploring their parents to stand by them.'

Maryam chuckled. 'Well, I often I see them close their eyes or fixate on a point. And then, they seem to take few deep breaths.'

Paul: 'They do. Deep breathing lowers their heart rate and is an effective way of releasing physical tension that could stand in the way of them giving it their best shot. And, they pay attention to their breathing, rather than to the many other things they could think of...'

Maryam: '...like "What if I fail?" or "What if we win?".'

Paul: 'Yes. And when they are quiet in that way, when they are still, they can bring all of who they are to the moment. That is much more important than what they know about the game intellectually.'

Maryam: 'So, they quieten their thoughts – their playlist – by shifting their attention. The thoughts may still be around, but can't affect them that much.'

Paul: 'Yes.'

Maryam: 'Because attention comes before awareness. I remember we spoke about that. We become more aware of the things we pay attention to. But we also become less aware of the things we don't pay attention to.'

Paul: 'This fundamental principle can be our friend on this journey. Your breath is the bridge that connects the world of your mind and body with the formless world of your true self, so they are not separate and you can leverage both.'

Maryam: 'Hmmm, you said you wanted me to have a short experience of something.'

Paul: 'Yes, would you mind if we did a small guided meditation together and talked about your experience afterwards?'

Maryam: 'Not at all. I'm curious. I don't think we have long, though – George and the kids will be back from the cinema soon.'

Paul: 'Oh, no worries. For the purpose of our conversation, a few minutes will suffice.'

Maryam: 'OK.'

Paul: 'First of all, I would like you to place your feet on the ground, sit up straight and comfortably. You can breathe much more easily when your tummy has more space.'

Maryam: 'OK.'

Both Maryam and Paul sat on the front of their chairs.[5] Paul spoke in a calm and peaceful, yet normal voice.

Paul: 'To start, simply take a few big, deep breaths – breathe in through your nose... hold it for a little moment... then breathe out gently through your mouth... OK... now take another deep breath...'

Both Maryam and Paul started breathing in this way. Maryam naturally closed her eyes without thinking about it.

Paul: 'Carry on, and allow yourself to breathe just a bit more slowly and deeply than you'd normally breathe...'

There was a pause...

Paul: 'Very good. Check in with you heart and notice how it's beating a little more slowly already...'

---

5   This brief example of a guided meditation is inspired by meditations taught by Thích Nhất Hạnh, Azim Khamisa and Andy Puddicombe, which I have integrated in my personal approach to meditation. I am practising variations based on how I feel, the time available, location, time of day, and my intention. There clearly is no right or wrong way of meditating, although certain practices have proven to be more helpful than others. I wholeheartedly recommend you explore headspace.com if you have a desire to integrate meditation into your daily life. (And no, I get no royalties for writing that.)

...

Paul: 'Carry on breathing through your nose... and allow your breath to settle into its natural rhythm.'

...

Paul: 'Check in with your body... notice how you feel...'

...

Paul: 'Now, on your next in-breath, I want you to silently remind yourself, "I'm aware of my in-breath" and "I'm aware of my out-breath". Just notice the rising and falling sensation of your breath.'

...

Paul: 'Breathing in: "aware"... breathing out: "aware"... feel it more than you think it.'

...

Paul: 'When thoughts come to your mind... like "Why are we doing this?" or "When will the kids be back?"... that's perfectly fine. Acknowledge them, and then allow them to move on, and bring your attention back to your breath...'

...

Paul: 'OK, at your next in-breath, silently say to yourself, "I'm aware of my breath" and on your out-breath say, "I'm enjoying my breath"... Breathing in: "aware", breathing out: "joy"...'

...

Paul: 'Check in with yourself...'

...

Paul: 'Now, during your next couple of breaths, I'd like you to focus your attention on your body... do a short body-scan starting with your head...'

...

Paul: '"I'm noticing my face... I'm noticing my neck... my shoulders... my arms... my heart... my back... my lower body... I'm aware of my legs... I'm aware of my feet".'

...

Paul: 'Notice any sensations in your body parts... notice any tensions or emotions. There's no need to change them... just acknowledge them.'

...

Paul: 'On your next in-breath, silently say to yourself, "I'm aware of my body"... Feel your body... and on your next out-breath, ask your body to help you release all tension, fear or worry... your body knows how to do that...'

...

Paul: 'Breathing in: "aware of body"... breathing out: "release".'

...

Paul: 'Breathing in: "aware"... breathing out: "release".'

...

Paul: 'Notice how you feel...'

...

Paul: 'Keep on breathing...'

...

Paul: 'Bring your attention back to your breath... and just notice how it's even calmer.'

...

Paul: 'Now, on your next in-breath, bring your attention to your heart space... breathe into your heart...'

...

Paul: 'As you breathe in and focus on you heart space, bring to mind a place where you feel at peace, were you feel a great sense of ease and joy... For me that is at the beach, overlooking the sea, feeling the waves washing over my feet, looking at the horizon...'

...

Paul: 'On your next couple of in-breaths, allow that picture to fill your heart with a warm sense of peacefulness... on your out-breath, release any feelings of worry, guilt or tension.'

...

Paul: 'Breathing in: "peace"... breathing out: "release".'

...

Paul: 'Check in with your body... notice this peacefulness... it's always available to you...'

...

Paul: 'Now I'd like you to bring your attention to your forehead, the spot just above your eyes. Do this very gently.'

...

Paul: 'Imagine there is a round window opening...'

...

Paul: 'You are now in a more quiet state... in a peaceful state...'

...

Paul: 'While you are there, put out a question that you'd like to find an answer to... or think of a goal that you have...'

...

Paul: 'Just put it out there... and then... let it go...'

...

Paul: 'Now, bring your attention back to you heart space. Keep on noticing your breathing...'

...

Paul: 'Before we close, I would like you to think of something that you feel genuinely grateful for... feel a deep sense of gratitude...'

...

Paul: 'In your own time, open your eyes, and make contact with your surroundings...'

Both Paul and Maryam sat quietly for a little while.

Paul: 'How do you feel?'

Maryam: '...Alive. It's like waking up after a good night's sleep on a Sunday morning, or the healthy sensation following a great workout. I feel... alert, but calm. Peaceful. Centred. Actually, I can't really put words to it. These are just labels. They don't quite capture it.'

Paul: 'Oh, that's alright. I feel your energy. What state of heart would you say you are in?'

Maryam: 'A calm one. There's calm energy in my heart space. I'm enjoying it. I'm happy.'

Paul: 'How does your mind feel? What's going on there?'

Maryam: 'Now it's quiet. But I must admit, at the beginning, I couldn't help thinking about things. I started by focusing on my breath, but at some stage I found myself solving problems. I was asking myself, "What if George comes back now, and we can't finish this?" and "Shouldn't we order a taxi to get you home?" Then, when I noticed I had lost focus on my breathing, I was a bit upset and said to myself, "Ahh, this is not the moment to do that. You can't even focus on a few breaths. C'mon, you don't want to disappoint Paul. He would like you to experience something here."'

Paul: 'Wonderful.'

Maryam: 'Why would that be *wonderful*?'

Paul: 'Because that's what I hoped you might experience.'

Maryam: 'I thought you wanted me to experience how we quieten our minds by focusing on our breathing.'

Paul: 'Yes, that's a part of it. And you've just had the experience of becoming aware of your stream of thoughts, your inner chatter.

There's nothing wrong with it. In the moment when you realised you were not focusing on your breath anymore, you became *aware* of your thoughts – you became *aware* of your autopilot. You took off your headphones and looked at the playlist. You even noticed how the playlist made you feel. When we are still, we can notice our stream of thoughts and the feelings they produce. On a blank canvas, we can observe the brushstrokes of our thoughts.'

Maryam: 'I became an observer of my own circle of energy.'

Paul: 'You were what is often called more mindful. You didn't only think, you were aware you were thinking. You didn't only feel, you were aware of your feeling.'

Maryam: 'And with awareness...'

Paul: '...comes choice. Strangely, we practice being present, by *not* being present. Then, when you notice you're not, you can choose to see and acknowledge the thought for what it really is – a thought. And you can choose to let go of the thought by not giving it further attention, by not entertaining it anymore. And then you brought your attention back to where you wanted it to be in that moment. Here, it happened to be your breath.'

'On a blank canvas, we can observe the brushstrokes of our thoughts.'

Maryam: 'I took charge of my iPod. In other words, being mindful simply means being aware of my playlist.'

Paul: 'Yes, and being conscious is the journey of reminding yourself that you are not the iPod, you are not your thoughts, but infinitely more. And there isn't necessarily anything "wrong" with your iPod or your playlist; your awareness just allows you to keep a bit of distance between you and your thoughts to remain an observer of your mind.'

Mindfulness: A Vaccine For Our Heart

There was a moment of quiet.

Maryam: 'Paul, George and the kids will be back soon, and I wanted to prepare a little snack for them. Would you mind coming into the kitchen with me to continue our conversation there?'

Paul: 'Oh, not at all. It's getting a little chilly as well, isn't it?'

Maryam: 'Yes, you're right. Would you like anything?'

Paul: 'A tea would be great, thank you, Maryam. And, where's your bathroom?'

Maryam showed Paul the way, then brought the cups and plates from the patio into the kitchen and started preparing some fresh fruit and berries.

Maryam, when Paul returned: 'Do you want some?'

Paul: 'Oh, you don't have to ask me twice, thank you. I just love berries, and they're coming into season. You'll see more berries on our menu soon.'

Maryam: 'Well, if I'm not travelling, you'll see me around.'

Maryam put some of the berries in a little bowl and handed it over to Paul.

Maryam: 'You know, our conversation today started with us talking about my *new room* where the happiness and energy of others becomes our *point of reference*. From that point of reference, leadership focuses on awakening the same qualities as true love. Mindfulness and presence are the doors to this room. I sense a much deeper understanding of what you truly meant when you first described our role as a Chief Energy Officer. I'm wondering even more now – how else, practically, can mindfulness help me to become a more effective Chief Energy Officer?'

Paul: 'That's a great question.' He paused for a moment. 'Why don't you imagine yourself in a, let's say, "difficult" meeting for a moment.'

Maryam: 'Alright.'

Paul: 'Can you bring to mind the people surrounding you, the topic that is on the table..., and also... the energy in the room?'

Maryam put aside the fruit in her hand and gazed out of the kitchen window.

Paul: 'Image the feeling in the room. Can you sense it?'

Maryam: 'Oh yes, for sure. I can feel the tension. I can feel my heart pounding right now. I feel the urge to say something.'

Paul: 'Is your state of heart more closed or open?'

Maryam: 'More closed. It's hardening, actually.'

Paul: 'What happens to your point of view right now? What about your ability to be influenced?'

Maryam: 'My views... they have become louder... in my head. I'm focusing on how to stand my ground.'

Paul: 'And as you feel this way, do the ideas you're having tend to be new and fresh, or more a replay of a store of memories?'

Maryam: 'Ah well, they are predominantly my previous thoughts, underpinned by more sharpened arguments.'

Paul: 'So when you feel and think this way, how much chance do you have of maintaining perspective in yourself and the state of heart of the others in the room?'

Maryam: 'I see your point.'

Paul: 'And that's as simple as it gets. For you to nurture healthy energies in others, you need to first be healthy and take care of yourself. And if it's mostly thoughts – the playlists – that affect the health of your heart, then returning to the here and now is like a vaccine. It helps your heart to remain healthy.'

Maryam: 'A vaccine for the heart? In which sense?'

Paul: 'Yes, our thoughts are such a wonderful tool. For example, they can imagine the future. They actually create it.'

Maryam: 'We wouldn't be able to create and invent anything without them.'

Paul: 'Indeed. Everything we as humans bring into existence, including this kitchen, was first a thought. But our thoughts can get stuck in a state of worry and fear about the future.'

'Being mindful is like a vaccine for your heart. It helps your heart to remain healthy.'

Maryam: 'I guess we all do that at times.'

Paul: 'I certainly do. Now, our thoughts can also remember the past...'

Maryam: 'That's how we learn, and avoid making mistakes more than five times.'

Paul, laughing: 'Yes, it can take more than one occasion to learn a lesson. So, we wouldn't go anywhere without this capacity of the mind, but our minds can get attached to limiting beliefs about ourselves and others, creating bitterness and judgments.'

Maryam: 'And these thoughts impact our state of heart in the present moment, and hence the present moment itself, right?'

Paul: 'Our thoughts are not a machine that we can just switch off, and we don't have to. We're always thinking, and as we've just seen, we are often thinking helpful thoughts. However, when we remember that we are not our thoughts, we are not the playlist, we can consciously keep a bit of a distance between our thoughts and ourselves. This tiny conscious space helps us to remain observers of our mind. It widens the space between our experiences, created by our thoughts, and our reactions. In my experience, people are more drawn to the space in us rather than to our actions. Does that resonate with your own experiences?'

'People are more drawn to the space in us than to our actions.'

Maryam: 'Yes, I can think of people who bring this space – this calm – to difficult situations. And this energy impacts on the people around them.'

Paul: 'Because we can feel others' energy, we are drawn to and impacted by a feeling of peace. It is often reflected in kind words and actions. My peace helps others to reconnect with their own innate peacefulness and kindness, and hence their energy.'

Maryam: 'I can see now what you mean by vaccine of the heart, but I guess you're not suggesting that I start meditating before and during board meetings, right?'

Paul, smiling: 'Well, it would be interesting to see what would happen if we did. I think it would transform our organisations. Until then, we might look at meditation more like a workout. If we work out in the morning, we feel more enlivened and fresh, even when we just sit in the office for the rest of the day.'

Maryam: 'That's true. The benefits of a workout continue after the workout itself. And the more regularly I work out, the more that sense of wellbeing persists.'

Paul: 'And in the same manner, the regular practice of meditation is an effective way to nurture mindfulness of your state of heart and your thoughts. Keep in mind that during our brief meditation, when you shifted your attention to your breathing and became aware of it, you did it all by yourself. You're born with the capacity to shift your awareness and the focus of your mind, just as you're born with muscles. In fact, young children are masters of letting go of thoughts.'

Maryam: 'That's so true. They worry, too, but just for a moment. And they can get upset, too, but just for a moment. If we don't intervene, they soon play joyfully again. And when they are that way, they radiate a magic energy that we adults would love to capture in a bottle to enjoy for ourselves. They really are teachers for living in the present moment.'

Paul: 'Well, given you and I were once children, we can trust we still have that ability inside of us at any time. When we meditate, we're just deliberately and consciously reconnecting with it. The practice of meditation simply helps us awaken and become more aware of that muscle of ours, so that over time we can more effortlessly access a mindful state and maintain it for a little longer throughout our day.

'For example, when you realise your playlist has taken over again, when you're talking to yourself, you can acknowledge it. Then a few conscious breaths can help you reconnect with your quiet state – the peacefulness you've experienced is always there for you to go to. Any time.'

Maryam: 'And I guess that includes board and project meetings.'

They laughed, looking at each other affectionately as if they were silently saying, 'Thank you for being here'.

Clearing the Slate and Compassionate Confrontation

Maryam took a plate from the cupboard above the sink and arranged the fruit on it, mixing in a few nuts.

Maryam: 'You know, Paul, I feel so peaceful and resourceful when we talk with each other like this. You're helping me reconnect with some truths that I've always been aware of, sources of energy that have always been there. And the reflection with you, your mere presence, impacts my state of heart. But then there's a voice inside me that keeps on saying, "Yeah, all well and good, but that's La La land." You see, when I go back to the office tomorrow, the reality is that there are problems – there are difficult relationships that impact on our work, there's history, there's politics involved, and, yes, there are some difficult characters.'

Paul listened attentively.

Maryam: 'And I know I'm making big judgments right now, and saying this in the light of all our conversations might sound as if they didn't matter to me, when actually they did. Believe me, they transformed me. I'm just trying to be realistic here, and acknowledge reality. I don't think there will ever be an organisation where there's no frustration or irritation, regardless of how mindful we are. Does that make sense at all?'

Paul: 'Completely. Actually, I'm wondering – can you think of *any* human organisation that you've experienced, be it a business, a family, or a school, where there's no tension or conflict at times?'

Maryam: 'Well, if you ask me that way... no.'

Paul: 'So, then, tension and conflict seem to be a part of our human nature.'

Maryam: 'It looks that way, yes.'

Paul: 'Whenever humans meet, they will step on each other's toes. Confrontation will happen. It is *human*. If you accept that, then the absence of conflict or tension is actually *not* a trait of a healthy team or organisation. Most of the time, people and organisations don't suffer from tension or conflict, unless of course it's a permanent state. They suffer from *avoiding trying to resolve it* while they still can. The choice we have is not between organisations with or without tension; the choice we have is whether we confront each other or not, and how we confront each other in ways that can heal our state of heart, transforming lower into higher vibrations.'

As Maryam listened to Paul, she was thinking of personal examples where she was experiencing low vibrations and avoiding conversations to resolve them.

'People in organisations don't suffer from tension or conflict. They suffer from avoiding trying to resolve it.'

Maryam: 'There are quite a few examples I can think of. There's one particular case with one of our leaders coming to mind.'

Paul: 'OK. Now, if you accept that we always do what makes sense to our heart so it can feel safe, why might avoiding such conversations make more sense to your heart than sharing how you felt?'

Maryam reflected. 'I guess, fundamentally, I want to keep the peace. And also avoid potential pain. Having this conversation would probably feel uncomfortable. And it doesn't feel safe at all.'

Paul: 'I understand. And what have you noticed about recent emails or conversations with that person?'

Maryam: 'Well, for a start, there have been fewer and fewer. We have avoided each other, I guess, to avoid the discomfort and the risk I just mentioned. And when we do speak, it's kind of cumbersome, clumsy, complicated. I am more worried about being misunderstood, so put preamble in front of almost everything I have to say: "Now, don't get me wrong here…" and things of that nature. And I avoid more difficult topics because I am worried the conversation will go south. Our working relationship has become less effective – we have lost time.'

Paul: 'OK, and how about your state of heart? Has it become more open or closed over time?'

Maryam: 'Well, she occupies a lot of space in my mind. Thinking about it, although we are speaking less often, ironically I find myself rolling my eyes over things I've heard about her more often. And I'm hearing more things. She is front of my mind. Do you see what I mean?' And that must happen hundreds of times throughout our organisation, every day. We step on each other's toes, as you said, and leave little bruises.'

Paul: 'Looking at this from the perspective of a CEO, we limit our access to the collective human energy available in our teams each time we don't reach out to "clear the slate", secretly hoping to avoid the pain that might come from doing so. What was at the start only a slight frustration can turn into bitterness. What was bitterness can turn into resentment. By this stage, we are so self-righteous that we have a hard time opening our hearts.'

Maryam: 'And that slows down the speed and quality of our conversations, like in my example. It reduces the enthusiasm, joy and energy we bring to our work. And that has a tangible price tag.'

Paul: 'Yes. I believe that feelings of resentment are among the strongest blocks to human energy in our organisations, families and societies. When we're feeling resentful, our state of heart is firmly closed and we can't bring all of our energy to the table anymore. The thoughts associated with resentment are strong forms of judgment and attachment to that judgment. They keep our state of heart firmly locked in its closed state, and we may even hurt ourselves without noticing it. When we feel resentment, we continue to feel superior to others, which gives us the illusion of control and safety, numbing our own suffering. Yet, it's like putting a patch over an infected wound. If it's not cleaned properly, the infection will get stronger. Nelson Mandela said, "Resentment is like drinking poison and then hoping it will kill your enemies".'

Maryam: 'And guilt?'

Paul: 'Well, guilt is basically resentment towards ourselves. We can't grow if we only see our mistakes as reaffirmations of our imperfections. And guilt puts us at the centre of our thoughts. The way I see it, our path to growth is not *blocked* by our and others' imperfections, it is *paved* by them; they *are* the path we're walking on. Without them, we can't grow. That's why our imperfections are so perfect.'

Maryam took a piece of fruit off the plate, and then sat down in front of Paul before she shared her next thought.

'Our path to growth is not blocked by our and others' imperfections, it is paved by them.'

Maryam: 'And forgiveness of others and ourselves reduces the luggage we carry while walking on this path.'

Paul: 'Ah, that speaks to me.'

With a gesture of her hand, Maryam invited Paul to taste some of the fruit on the plate.

Paul: 'Now, have you ever been in situations where you and someone else overcame your resistance to confronting each other, and as a result of you both doing so, and seeking to understand each other's views and motives, your relationship became stronger and more trusting?'

Maryam: 'Oh yes. The first relationship coming to mind is actually my marriage. But I can think of a few business examples as well. Whether that happened or not depended, in my experience, on *how* we confronted each other.'

Paul: 'Tell me more.'

Maryam: 'Well, it depended on how I felt inside when I reached out. It was less a matter of my rhetorical abilities.'

Paul: 'That's interesting. You see, my sense is that every time we feel hurt by someone, with or without the other person's intention or knowledge, it leaves a tiny streak on our glasses. If we don't occasionally clean our glasses, these streaks accumulate on our lenses.'

Maryam: 'So we can't see clearly anymore. What we see is actually distorted.'

Paul: 'Yes, that's what I mean. Forgiveness is not an act or a smart method. It's a *practice*, a *state of mind*, something we might need to do dozens of times during a day. When we practise with mundane things, like letting go of an unkind word someone has said to us, we can be more prepared when the big things happen.'

Maryam paused before replying, and Paul waited. He could sense both peacefulness and confusion emerging in her.

Maryam: 'I can see that. But then, as leaders, we face many different things we can't simply deny or permit, condone or give in to.'

Paul took a sip of water. 'Let me ask you this. In light of our last conversation, what would you say is the single most powerful human thought habit that can block our energy?'

Maryam allowed her thoughts to wander back to the last conversation with Paul.

Maryam: 'I'd say dualistic thinking and judgment. They often co-create the very outcomes we are judging.'

Paul: 'If we consider judgment to be the single most important barrier to an open state of heart, then the capacity of suspending or letting go of our judgments when they occur is vital to *transforming* energy first in ourselves, then in others. Now, resentment and guilt are basically very strong forms of judgment, and we can become quite attached to them. When we feel resentful or guilt, things then look "true". It seems to me that transformation and growth are more often the result of *subtracting* rather than *adding* beliefs that we have turned into truths...'

'Transformation and growth are the result of subtracting rather than adding beliefs.'

Maryam: '...because the cork has all it needs to float back to the surface on its own.'

Paul: 'Yes, you could say that. The people you lead have all they need to revert to an open state of heart. And that brings us back your question.

'In the first place, forgiveness is not something you do for *others* – you do it for *yourself*. Forgiveness is the practice of acknowledging, accepting, and then letting go of the thoughts and feelings that close *your* heart. You don't need others to do to that. Forgiving is not denying, nor condoning. But how can you serve others when you are in a closed state of heart? I would suggest that being forgiving helps you to confront yourself and others more effectively. You could say it allows you to see more clearly.'

Maryam: 'Well, if you look at business this way, then forgiveness would be a central leadership skill so we can keep perspective more often.'

Paul: 'Maybe the practice of forgiveness is one of the single most important skills of a CEO. What would be the alternative?'

Maryam: 'A closed state of heart and a dirty pair of glasses. Sounds like a recipe for disaster and suffering.'

Paul laughed while holding up both hands. 'Oh yes, I can think of quite a few moments when I was just like that. You see – I'm not suggesting that conflict is fun or easy, nor that there is a simple recipe for overcoming it. Not at all. Forgiveness is work, and it's messy.

'Maybe the practice of forgiveness is one of the single most important skills of a CEO.'

What I'd invite you to consider is that tension continues to be an obstacle, if you see it that way. If you choose to see and *accept* tension as an opportunity to transform closed states of heart into more open ones, then you might embrace it more often and, over time, strengthen the energy in the organisation.'

Maryam was quiet for a moment.

Maryam: 'I don't know if this belongs here, but I'd like to share an experience I recently had with my son.'

Paul: 'Oh, I'd love to hear that.'

Maryam: 'I had an argument with Daniel. It started about some feedback I got from his teacher about his performance at school. She wasn't all that happy with his participation and his attitude. Of course, I wanted to ask him about this as soon as we got home.

'When I did, saying, "Hey, son, I want to talk with you about some feedback I got from Mrs Johnston", he reacted strongly and in a very defensive manner. For me, this was a confirmation that there must be some truth in what I had heard. He ran into his room, slamming the door and shouting things like "Nobody understands me. You are just like her. Leave me alone".

'While I wasn't surprised that he didn't want to talk about it, I did react to the intensity of his tone and words. So I ran after him. My heart was pounding. I opened the door to his room and told him that I found his attitude unacceptable. Well, in all truth, my voice rose and I threatened him, saying, "If you say something like that one more time..." and things of that nature. Of course, that didn't make it better. He must have felt threatened, and small, and guilty, and I guess that was secretly my intention, upset as I was.

'The whole thing got out of control – we were both out of control. My heart was racing and I felt so sad. We looked at each other like enemies, and seeing that look in his eyes, knowing he was seeing a similar look in my eyes at that moment, was so painful, it was heart-breaking. We could only see disappointment in each other.

I don't think either of us could believe we were doing this to one another, yet we couldn't change it.

'And then, suddenly, everything changed. For a brief moment when I looked at him, I didn't see my disappointment but his suffering. I took him in my arms, pressed him against my chest and said, "I'm sorry, Daniel, I'm just so afraid." The words just poured out of my mouth.

'In the same moment, Daniel relaxed in my arms and we both cried. He sobbed and whispered into my ear, "You don't need to be afraid, Mum. I love you." The moment was so intense – we looked into each other's eyes and our expressions had completely changed. Seconds before, we'd felt alienated and unforgiving; now we were closer than we had been in a long time. It was completely disarming.'

Maryam's eyes welled up with tears as she recounted the events, and Paul felt like getting up and taking her into his arms.

Paul: 'What happened in that moment?'

Maryam: 'I don't know. It's a bit of a mystery to me. You could say we both forgave each other, but in the moment itself, it wasn't any more necessary to forgive, to *do* something. It just happened. Somehow, I surrendered; we surrendered.'

They sat in silence.

Paul: 'I think you both surrendered to the abundant love inside you. That's what you experienced. There's no value in describing it, but from your experience you can trust that you have the innate capacity to love. You transformed the energy, right?'

Maryam: 'Yes, we did.'

Paul: 'Your love *is* forgiving, and forgiving *is* love. And true leadership is love. It's not always accessible, but it's always available.'

He paused.

Paul: 'The way I see it, conflict and tension, small or big, can be paths towards more unity, if we choose to look at it that way. And forgiveness – is the *gateway*.'

Maryam: 'Gateway?'

Paul: 'Let me ask you this. Have you ever snapped at someone?'

Maryam: 'Oh yeah, often.'

Paul: 'And when that happens, why does it make sense to you in the moment to snap? What's going on for you?'

Maryam: 'It typically happens when I feel insecure or when "I'm falling", as I call it sometimes. It's in moments when I realise that I'm losing control over the outcome. It's in moments when what someone else thinks or does is really getting in the way of what I would like to achieve. And I would say it tends to happen when I'm already in a closed state of heart for some reason.'

Paul: 'I don't think you're alone with that. Now, imagine you'd waited until your state of heart was open again, when it was peaceful again, and then instead of not talking about whatever had made you snap, trying to avoid the feeling of embarrassment you were anticipating, you had leaned in. You had gone to see your colleague and said something along the lines of, "Hey, do you have a moment? Please forgive me for the tone of our conversation earlier. I felt under pressure, and then I just snapped. This happens when I sense that I'm losing control or feel overwhelmed. I'm aware of that. I'm a work in progress". What do you think you doing this would have done for the state of heart of the other?'

Maryam: 'Hmm, I think the chances are it would have opened. It would have healed the damage that was caused and reduced the likelihood that this disagreement would continue in their mind during the evening. Instead of talking with others about the moment I snapped, he would have been thinking and talking about the moment when I reached out and how that felt.'

Paul: 'And how might it have felt for you?'

Maryam: 'The same. I guess, it would have felt liberating. I'd have been able to move on.'

Paul: 'Asking for forgiveness and speaking truth can instantly transform a low-energy into a high one because it is rooted in a high-vibration energy – a more loving energy.'

Maryam: 'So forgiveness and speaking truth are part of the CEO toolbox, right?'

Paul: 'Well, as a CEO, you commit to transforming energy. And you're starting with the assumption that this capacity is available to you. In business, we usually only need a tiny fraction of the love and forgiveness that was available to you in the situation with your son. But we might need this fraction *frequently* during the day, if you see what I mean?'

Maryam: 'I think I do. In fact, most of the time we're not talking about anything major – typically no one dies. But it's the many small things we do that affect others and can cause irritation or bother – one email at a time. And if left hanging, these feelings accumulate and create a reality of their own.'

Paul: 'That's what I mean. To use your language – we are transforming energy one conversation at a time, one email at a time, one meeting at a time.'

'We are transforming energy one conversation at a time, one email at a time, one meeting at a time.'

Maryam: 'I have an example, a colleague of mine who comes to mind. Are you OK if we talk about him? You don't know him.'

Paul: 'Sure.'

Maryam: 'I'll call him Jonathan – it's not his real name. Recently, he's done a few things that I really don't understand. For example, he's delayed doing his part in executing a programme everyone else has bought into. And while he keeps on telling me that he supports it, I know for a fact he's been sending emails asking his team not to send anyone on the programme until further notice from him. In short, he's sabotaging what we're doing.'

Paul: 'How does that make you feel?'

Maryam: 'Angry is the simplest way of putting it. I feel hurt.'

Paul: 'I can understand that. And, by saying that out loud, you've taken the first step towards possibly forgiving him. By that, I don't mean you're condoning what he might be doing.'

Maryam: 'So what is it then?'

Paul: 'Acceptance. Like in the moment with your son, you are *accepting* that you feel hurt. You are acknowledging that your state of heart is closing as you're thinking of him. When you can say, "I feel hurt", you're accepting life as it is, rather than rejecting it. Imagine if you said to yourself, "It's all OK", trying to ignore the feeling that you don't want to have or believe you're not supposed to have.'

Maryam looked surprised. 'I didn't consider that.'

Paul: 'There's not necessarily anything you have to do about your feeling of hurt at the moment, but you could simply acknowledge that anger is a seed that is in you; it's part of your playlist. You are the one noticing it...'

Maryam, smiling: '...as a matter of fact.'

Paul: 'Do you mind if I ask you a few questions about Jonathan?'

Maryam: 'Not at all.'

Paul: 'All I'd like you to do is notice your state of heart as you are answering them, alright?'

Maryam: 'Sure.'

Paul: 'Is it possible that, just like you, Jonathan is trying to feel happy in his life?'

Maryam: 'Yes.'

Paul: 'Do you believe that, just like you, Jonathan wants to feel safe and avoid pain in his life?'

Maryam: 'Yes.'

Paul: 'Can you accept that, just like you, Jonathan has done things because he felt afraid or hurt?'

Maryam: 'Surc.'

Paul: 'Would you agree that, just like you, Jonathan has probably experienced sadness, loss, or loneliness in his life? And would you agree that, just like you, Jonathan doesn't want to make anyone suffer; he's doing what he thinks he has to do to feel happy and safe.'

Maryam: 'Yes. I agree. Of course.'

Paul paused, and they both remained silent for a few moments.

Paul: 'What have you noticed about your state of heart?'

Maryam: 'It opened a little bit each time I thought of him this way.'

Paul: 'Like with your son, you have changed your point of reference. You've recognised yourself in him. You've recognised that if you had his life, you would do the same thing. You've recognised that if he *could* have acted otherwise, he *would* have. Everything he does is logical – it's *psycho*-logical.'

Maryam: 'It made sense to his frightened heart.'

Paul: 'Probably. We don't know for sure. This mindset, and the feeling that comes with it, is what we call compassion. As soon as you tap into that mindset, your capacity to forgive naturally comes forward.'

Maryam: 'OK, but I still disagree with what he's doing.'

Paul: 'Of course. You don't need to agree to open you heart, but you might have to open your heart to be able to agree, or at least to understand to start with.'

'You don't need to agree to open your heart. You might have to open your heart to be able to agree.'

Maryam: 'And if he doesn't have an open state of heart?'

Paul: 'That's very likely, I guess, but irrelevant.'

Maryam: 'Why is that irrelevant? When his state of heart is closed, he's less likely to have a productive conversation.'

Paul: 'Oh, that's for sure. Well, take the example with your son. Were his feelings a condition for your change of heart?'

Maryam: 'No. It was quite the opposite.'

Paul: 'Compassion and forgiveness are an inside job. As we said, you're first doing it for yourself, not for anyone else. And, at the same time, the other person cannot *not* feel you.'

Maryam: 'In other words, how I feel inside impacts on our conversation more than what I have to say.'

Paul: 'So-called "relationship problems" are often just relationships seen through a closed state of heart.'

Maryam's phone rang.

Maryam: 'Forgive me, Paul, let me just take this. It's George... Hi, honey...'

Leading from the soul: intuition and inspiration

Maryam hung up the phone. 'After the cinema, they ran into friends of ours who had also been watching a movie with their kids, so they decided to get ice cream together, but now they're stuck in traffic. He thinks they'll be here in another twenty minutes or so. He was asking if you would mind if he drove you home afterwards.'

Paul: 'Oh, I can take a taxi. George has had a long day.'

Maryam: 'I insist. Allow us to take you home.'

Paul: 'OK, thank you. That's very kind of you and George.'

Maryam: 'You're so welcome, Paul. Given we have a few minutes left, I would love to explore another question that has been puzzling me from our last conversation.'

Paul: 'Oh, I love puzzling thoughts.'

Maryam: 'Essentially, last time we talked about the value of suspending judgment to make judgment calls.'

Paul: 'Yes, you could say that.'

Maryam: 'How might this notion of mindfulness that we talked about help me make better judgment calls?'

Paul: 'Ah, thank you Maryam. That's such a wonderful question. Let's look at this in a different way. Just see if the following is true for you, and let me know if not, OK?'

Maryam: 'Sure.'

Paul: 'Would you agree that you are probably more than your body, feelings and thoughts?'

Maryam: 'We talked about this earlier today. I don't know for sure and I never will, but most philosophies, spiritual traditions or theologies on this planet seem to have a notion of soul, spirit, consciousness or God – something that transcends our material existence.'

Paul: 'Let me ask the question more bluntly. Do you have a soul?'

At first, Maryam was a bit puzzled as Paul usually asked questions in a gentle, explorative way, but his voice was so kind, she could feel the care embedded in his question.

Maryam: 'Well, if you ask it in this manner, yes. Yes, I have a soul.'

Paul: 'Now, regardless of what you call it – soul, consciousness, or God – and regardless of what you believe in, would you agree that all these dimensions of our existence, if I can call them that for a moment, are intangible for us and probably infinite?'

Maryam: 'Yes, I think they have that in common.'

Paul: 'And would you consider that most of what we experience as humans – our bodies, our physical sensations, our behaviours and actions – are tangible and finite?'

Maryam: 'Yes. We can see them. We can measure them.'

Paul: 'So, where would you fit our thoughts in?'

Maryam: 'Hmm, that's a tricky one. They are somewhere in between. They are intangible as I can't touch them, but I can measure them – they are electrical signals. And then, if I think anything, my thoughts can go anywhere.'

Paul: 'OK. And when you have a new thought – not a memory, a fresh thought you didn't have before – where would you say your thought started?'

Maryam: 'In my brain. In one or many of my synapses.'

Paul: 'So, did your synapse have the thought? Where exactly in the synapse do you think it started? What triggered the electron that later became what we call a thought to move?'

Maryam: 'That I don't know.'

Paul: 'I don't know either. Nowadays we know much more about how and where we store and retrieve information in our brains, and which parts are active when we experience things and make decisions. We also know that we think and know much more than we can express in conscious thoughts or language. Yet we can't really tell where our new thoughts originate. But let me ask you this – how would something as infinite and wise as your soul communicate with something finite like your body?'

Maryam: 'I'm not sure. But maybe it has something to do with our thoughts, which seem to be in between.'

Paul: 'I think you are right. In a sense, our thoughts are the first materialisation of something completely intangible. You see, it seems to me that these two realities of our existence, our immaterial infinite dimension and our material finite dimension, are not separate. I prefer to see them as two poles of the same reality that ranges from our intangible nature, our consciousness, to our tangible nature, our actions. Our thoughts and the feelings they create are the bridge between them.'

Maryam: 'Our thoughts would then not only be a re-combination of already existing thoughts, ideas and information, but also a gate to our soul?'

Paul: 'Yes. The quiet thoughts. We can know more than we can know about.'

Maryam: 'Well, let's assume for a moment that was the case, how would that awareness help me practically to make better judgments and decisions in my daily work?'

Paul: 'Allow me to ask the question differently. If you could ask your soul for advice, would you take it?'

Maryam: 'Yes, I think so. It's been around a little longer than my brain, so it has a different vantage point. And – given it's my true self – it is probably fond of me.'

Paul, giggling: 'So, if you accept that to be true, how could you listen to your soul? How could you make choices that are aligned with what your soul would do? How could you tap into this wisdom to make better decisions or better choices?'

Maryam: 'I don't know.'

Paul: 'I don't know either. But I do know that 95% of what we sense, think and know is unconscious before some of it may eventually become part of our conscious awareness. We know, we sense, more than we can consciously think, let alone express in words. Yet we tend to attribute a lot of value to the remaining 5%, which is our intellect.'

Maryam: 'Hmmm, from a business perspective, I'm wondering, then, how to access the 95% more often to make better use of the remaining 5%?'

Paul: 'I believe your soul speaks to you all the time – just very quietly. It whispers. You might not hear it. Sometimes the more noisy 5% – the inner chatter, the words you're thinking – gets your attention. But, when you're still, you can notice the feelings and sensations your soul creates. You could say that your *state of heart* reflects the wisdom of your soul. It's like a bridge to your soul. Your feelings are maybe the first material manifestation of an immaterial truth.'

Maryam: 'Hmm, I hadn't looked at my heart as a bridge. But how can I be sure this is the case?'

Paul: 'Well, as a matter of fact, you can't be sure until you die. I'm not asking you to agree with me. The question for me is more, "How would I act, if my state of heart reflects the wisdom of my soul, if I allowed it to inform my choices?"'

Maryam: 'But what if there is no such thing as a soul?'

Paul: 'I would suggest you would have nothing to lose. And, if you prefer, you could explain the value of listening to your state of heart from a scientific neurological perspective. For me, these are different doors to the same place. Your right brain and your limbic brain communicate with you through moods and feelings, allowing you to understand things and make choices way before you can explain them or express them in language. That's what we call intuition. So, whether you accept a neurological or a spiritual stance, taking your state of heart seriously seems like an effective path. Personally, I find that both perspectives are complementary and don't exclude each other at all. Either way, if we learn to listen to our intuition more fully, we're using the full capacity of our senses, our brains, and possibly the wisdom of our souls.'

Maryam: 'Sounds like a good deal to me.'

Paul: 'So, either way, you can rely on your state of heart as a guide for both the quality of your thoughts and the wisdom of your soul.

If your heart is open, it's more likely you're being who you truly are. You can trust your conscious thoughts and your intuition. If it's closed, your soul can't be the one talking, as it never judges. It can't be universal truth, only personal truth. It might even be someone else talking.'

Maryam: 'And who would that be?'

Paul: 'That's a good question. I don't know. Could be "learned voices" from parents, school, work, society that are not aligned with who you want to be, who you truly are any more. Instead, they make up the image you've created of yourself, beliefs that look like truths.'

> 'You can rely on your state of heart as a guide for both the quality of your thoughts and the wisdom of your soul.'

Maryam: 'I think I know these voices. I'm wondering, though, how I can distinguish them from my soul's voice.'

Paul: 'I can't tell you that. That's something you'll need to find out for yourself over time. I've learned that one of the central things the United States Navy SEALs practise and learn over their many years of training is not when to shoot, but when *not* to shoot.[6] In a sense, suspending judgment means learning when *not* to talk or react when your first thought comes. Sometimes you just have to wait.'

Maryam: 'Wait? For what?'

Paul: 'Well, maybe "be still" is a better way of putting it. Choose to be still until you feel that what you are thinking or about to say comes from an open state of heart. You might quietly check in

---

6   Source: *Stealing Fire: How Silicon Valley, the Navy SEALs, and Maverick Scientists Are Revolutionizing the Way We Live and Work*, Steven Kotler and Jamie Wheal

with yourself and ask, "Do I feel *inspired* by what I'm going to say or do?" If so, if you're coming from that place – and you don't need to understand why – you're probably being guided by truth and wisdom. In order to *know*, we sometimes need to first empty ourselves of what we know, our stored wisdom. It could take a few conscious breaths to create that space from where clarity comes. Or it could take longer.'

Maryam, taking a deep breath: 'We spoke about this before, didn't we? You called this practice "taste your words and taste your feelings".'

Paul: 'Yes.'

Maryam: 'What would happen if I came from this inspired place a little bit more often?'

Paul: 'What do you think would happen?'

Maryam: 'Given that talking is fundamentally what leaders do for a living – it's certainly my main tool – I might inspire people, affect their state of heart, or quite simply bring clarity to a situation more often.'

Paul: 'Yeah, that could happen. Out of curiosity, can you think of people who have inspired you in your life?'

Maryam: 'Oh yes, quite a few. Some are friends, some are people I have worked with, and some are famous people I've heard or read about.'

Paul: 'As you're thinking about these people, what would you say they have in common that nurtures a sense of inspiration in you?'

Maryam thought about some of the people who had touched her in her life. She was looking at their faces as if they were in front of her.

Maryam: 'It's not so much something specific they have said or done, although they have said or done things that have moved me. Sometimes, it's their journey and what they have realised over time. It's more... what they stand for. They seem to be clear on why they are doing what they are doing. They all see meaning in what they are doing. And what they do becomes an expression of this sense of meaningfulness. Some of them are able to express it in words, while some are not, but it seems they are all focused on serving in some shape or form.

'For example, a friend of mine is a mother of two young children, and I find it's magic to experience her in that role. She has amazing patience and care when she's baking cakes with the kids, even when there's chaos everywhere. Sometimes she lets them discover the ingredients and how to use them. The thoughtfulness that goes into the children's birthday parties she hosts – everyone is full of joy. The attention to detail she brings when preparing the house for Christmas and Easter with the kids, and so on.

'One day, I asked her, "Why do you do all these things? You have so much else to do, and I can see you're tired." Do you know what she said?'

Paul: 'I'm curious.'

Maryam: 'She said, "I know I'm probably doing too much, but it's my way of expressing love. I would like my children to experience my love in ways they will remember and pass on one day. That's why." You see, deep in her heart, she knows her why. That gives her this abundant infectious energy, although she is not a loud person, if you see what I mean?'

Paul waited a moment before responding.

Paul: 'You have that same capacity. You bring it forward every time you listen to your soul and speak from that place. Then you are tapping into the abundant energy that is there for yourself and for others. And that is what CEOs truly do.'

The front door opened. George and the children had arrived home. Maryam and Paul stood and hugged, and Maryam gently whispered, 'Thank you, my friend. You are a gift in my life.'

'So are you,' replied Paul.

They talked for a bit with George and the kids about the film and the time they'd spent with their friends, then George took Paul home. After they'd left, Maryam grabbed her notebook and looked at the circle of energy. She reflected for a moment, and then added a note.

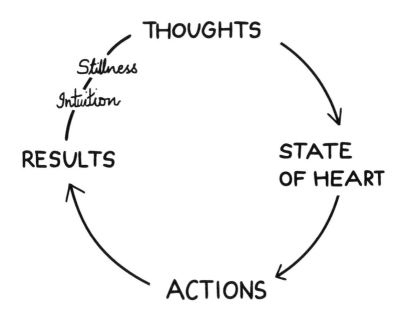

Journaling

Maryam went to bed early that Sunday. The next day, she got up before everyone else. It was still dark outside. She felt fresh and truly rested. Maryam had a late morning flight to catch. She knew it would be a busy week, and that she might not find an appropriate moment to reflect and journal her thoughts, which had become such a precious practice. So, she had decided to jot down the thoughts that had emerged from yesterday's dinner before her taxi arrived to pick her up. The quiet gentle energy in and around the house felt like an open invitation to contemplate.

Maryam felt like starting her day with the same kind of short meditation practice that Paul had introduced her to yesterday. She remembered that she felt centred and focused after only a few breaths. She was committed to start practising meditation, and simply decided that this practice would start right now.

Maryam closed her eyes and took few deep breaths. She loved doing that. She started breathing a bit more slowly, more consciously and she noticed her breath. After a moment she enjoyed her breathing. And, as she continued just for a little longer, Maryam noticed that it wasn't her doing the breathing, she was witnessing it. Her breathing could take care of itself.

After few minutes only Maryam brought her attention back to the room. It was still very quiet. There was more light coming into the room now and she felt alive. She started writing the thoughts that were there for her.

Leadership:

- comes from and nurtures the same qualities as love.

- happens when I shift my point of reference – from myself to others.

Humans:

- are actually warm and fluffy.

- have two fundamental needs: to feel loved and avoid pain.

- And when people do things that are unhealthy or hurtful, chances are they don't feel loved or are afraid.

Presence:

- is a vaccine for my heart.

- We learn being present by (noticing when we are) *not* being present.

- I am the pilot. Once I notice my autopilot is activated, I can switch it off.

- I am not my iPod. I'm the one using it. I am not my thoughts, I am the one using them.

Conflict and Forgiveness:

- The absence of tension is not a differentiating trait of healthy organisations; the ability to resolve it and heal is.

- Resentment and guilt are strong forms of judgment and as such among the biggest obstacles to accessing our higher forms of energy.

- We limit access to human energy each time we choose to not reach out and 'clear the slate'.

- Conflict is actually not an impediment to compassion, yet a possible gateway.

- In the same way, our path of growth is not limited by our imperceptions it is paved by it.

- I don't need to agree in order to open my heart, yet I probably have to open my heart in order to be able to agree.

- Forgiveness transforms energy. Maybe the practice of forgiveness is one of the most essential capabilities of a Chief Energy Officer. This too is an innate capacity.

Soul:

- I am not my thoughts, just as I am not my eyesight. I am the one who is aware I'm having thoughts. I am infinitely more. So are all the others.

- Maybe our thoughts, when they occur in a very open state of heart, are our bridge to higher wisdom.

- We can use our state of heart as a way to communicate with our higher wisdom when we dig deep to make difficult choices. When we feel inspired by a choice, a thought, an idea, or a hunch, it's a powerful clue. And vice versa.

- Whether it's our soul or 'only' the unconscious 95% of our brain and body talking, we'll find out later. It's definitely more than our limited 5% conscious mind. Let's not waste resources and use what we've been given.

- What would happen if we chose to be guided by our sense of inspiration more often?

CHAPTER 6

Body: Action Through Doing And Being

'Action by itself is blind, reflection impotent.'

Mihaly Csikszentmihalyi

'We are not human beings having a spiritual experience.
We are spiritual beings having a human experience.'

Pierre Teilhard de Chardin

'Silence is the language of God, all else is poor translation.'

Rumi

After spending the day at Maryam's home, Paul didn't see her for quite a while. She was too busy visiting clients, colleagues, and her team members in several of the locations she oversaw. She only got to the office at the end of the week to sit down with her assistant to share updates with each other, plan the week ahead, and sign a few documents. She didn't feel a desire to reach out to Paul during these weeks; rather, she felt a need to pause and let things happen naturally.

Maryam had downloaded a book on meditation and started building moments of quiet into her morning and evening routines. She had also found an app with guided meditations that she found useful to help her discover additional ways of approaching her moments of quiet, increasingly finding that she preferred not being guided. At times, when she was travelling, or moments before a meeting, she enjoyed sitting in her chair and focusing on her breathing. Sometimes she even did it during meetings, and no one but she would notice.

The afternoon with Paul had affected Maryam in a way she couldn't articulate, but she clearly felt it. Something in her had pivoted. It was like a silent yet potent wave of aliveness pouring throughout her body. Her husband noticed a shift in her, and one evening he asked her to share how she was feeling and what was happening.

Maryam: 'George, it's strange. All I can say is that I feel more peaceful and whole. But it is difficult to explain why that is. Even if I could explain it eloquently, it wouldn't reflect what is truly going on. And I don't know why, but I don't enjoy talking about it. I'm enjoying the experience... I'm so sorry, darling, I guess I'm not making any sense here.'

A few colleagues approached her, some openly sharing how much they appreciated the fact that she had joined the organisation and how much they enjoyed working with her. Others just hung around in her vicinity or sought her opinion more often. It happened more regularly that the team spontaneously decided to have lunch together or go out for a quick dinner. While there were still as many challenges and demands as ever to cope with, and she didn't feel like she was doing anything in particular differently, she couldn't help but notice that she wasn't experiencing as much wear and tear as she had before she'd started talking with Paul.

Maryam was also receiving applications from various colleagues who wanted to join her department. This was most refreshing, since she used to have great difficulties keeping colleagues, in spite of the salary increases and other material benefits she had offered. Sometimes, she now received support from colleagues when she least expected it; it just happened.

While she had no explanation for it, she knew in her heart all of these changes were related to her journey. It felt as if she had taken a new path without even realising it, but it didn't matter. She was grateful for having found a new friend. Somehow she had thought that people didn't make new friendships at her age.

She got up on the Monday after her last work trip and arrived at the office earlier than usual to beat the traffic and catch up on some emails. To her surprise, she saw Paul and a few of his team members jogging across the court in front of the main entrance.

Paul spotted her, stopped his running and walked towards her, waving to the others and saying, 'Carry on, I'll see you in a moment, OK?'

Paul: 'Hi, Maryam, good to see you. Looks like you've been away for a while.'

Maryam: 'Good to see you too, Paul. Yes, I've been travelling quite a bit and came in early today to catch up with things.'

Paul: 'I thoroughly enjoyed the time we spent together at your house. I'd like to thank you and George again for your hospitality and a special day.'

Maryam: 'Oh, the pleasure was all ours, Paul. But, hey, I don't want to stop you from running.'

Paul: 'We were just about to finish. I've had a good run.'

Maryam: 'I must admit... I'm a little bit surprised to see you working out in the morning.'

Paul: 'Oh, why?'

Maryam: 'Well, to be honest, after our last conversation about states of heart and soul, I didn't picture you with trainers on and a sweatband around your head, but more sitting on a chair, quietly reflecting. Forgive me, though. I feel a bit embarrassed saying that now.'

When Paul chuckled in his heart-warming way, Maryam knew he wasn't offended at all.

Paul: 'Well, I am my soul... in a material and increasingly aging body. So, if I don't take care of it, chances are I will have fewer opportunities to do the things I care about. Do you go running?'

Maryam: 'Yes, usually in the evenings. I find it easier to make time then, and it helps me sleep better.'

Paul: 'Well, next time you do it, try to be depressed or irritated.'

Maryam, laughing: 'Why would I do that?'

Paul: 'Because it won't work. You see, our body and mind are one in so many ways, I sometimes wonder why we came up with different words for them. For example, when I feel physically well, I find that my mind is more focused, and I tend to be in an open state of heart naturally. I even find it easier to meditate. And when my mind is in a healthy state, I have more physical energy and the desire get things done, or try new things. There is a time for everything, as many wise people have said[7] – a time for action and a time for stillness.'

Maryam: 'Speaking of which, I guess we'd better both get on.'

Paul: 'Indeed, otherwise there will be a whole bunch of hungry people today. I was wondering... would you like to join the team and me for lunch? We usually eat when everything is quiet and cleaned up at around 2:30. You'll probably be busy today, but what about tomorrow? I would love to introduce you to a few people on my team.'

Maryam: 'Excellent idea. I would love to.'

Paul: 'See you at 2.30?'

Maryam: 'Tomorrow at 2.30 it is.'

---

7   Ecclesiastes 3: 'There is a time for everything'; Lao Tzu: 'There's a time for everything, and everything in its time'.

Inspiration: soul decisions

Maryam arrived at the restaurant the next day at the agreed time, meeting a few of her colleagues coming back from their lunch break. They all seemed to be in a good mood, chatting, enjoying the walk.

When she entered the restaurant, she immediately noticed the smell of cinnamon. It reminded her of a dessert her mum used to prepare; the smell warmed her inside. She then spotted a large brown panel over the counter.

THIS WEEK: CELEBRATING SCENTS OF CINNAMON

Bring your grandma's recipe.

We'll cook the top 10 for everyone.
OK, we'll take Mum's recipe too. And we'll take
Dad's as well, but only if it's le-gen-da-ry.

Maryam couldn't help but smile and shake her head in amusement. Not only did she like cinnamon, but she also loved the light-hearted tone, reminding her of the first time she'd experienced this place. She loved the idea of the restaurant involving its customers and inviting them to become co-creators of the menu; she had never experienced anything like that before.

She spotted Paul at a table at the back, sitting with some of his colleagues. He waved his hand, inviting her to come over. As she came closer, Paul stood up to welcome her.

Maryam: 'Hi, Paul. Hi, everyone. I'm Maryam. Nice to meet you.'

Paul: 'Maryam, I'm glad you could make it. Team, it's my pleasure to introduce you to Maryam, our Head of Business Development for Emerging Markets and a dear friend.'

Everyone greeted Maryam, who went around the table shaking hands, trying hard to remember the names of the team members who were there: Joseph, Sue, Roberta, Ahmed and Deepa.

Paul: 'I had the pleasure of eating at Maryam's house a few weeks ago, and although I hope, Maryam, I will have the honour of cooking for you and your family at my house one day, maybe today my team and I can treat you to a few things we've kept back for you.'

Maryam: 'Oh, thank you, Paul, thank you, everyone, for having me. What can I say? It smells wonderful.'

Paul: 'Maryam is interested in our work here, so I thought it would be wonderful to share a few of our thoughts and experiences with her during our lunch. In the end, sharing is an essential part of eating, isn't it?'

Everybody smiled and nodded. They served one another and started eating. Maryam tried cannelloni in an asparagus sauce. To her surprise, she tasted a tiny bit of cinnamon. She hadn't expected it. And she loved it.

Paul: 'I know, it's unusual, isn't it? It's an idea from an Italian colleague; I think he's in Finance.'

Joseph: 'Yes, Giuseppe. It's a recipe from his mum in Sicily. It went straight into the top 10.'

Maryam: 'I wanted to ask you about that. Who came up with the idea of collecting recipes from your guests?'

Sue: 'I'm not sure anymore who had this specific idea, but it was born during one of our "joy of life" sessions and we've loved doing it. We'll probably do it more regularly because of the positive response we got.'

Maryam: 'What is a joy of life session?'

Roberta: 'We simply gather together every other week for an hour or so and think about how else we could express our sense of purpose: "celebrating and nurturing the joy of life through great food and togetherness".'

'The questions we ask ourselves matter. They shape what we give attention and energy to. They plant seeds and nurture them.'

Maryam remembered that Paul had mentioned his team's purpose during their first encounter, and that contributing to that purpose was what gave him and the team... life.

Maryam: 'Is it that simple?'

Roberta: 'Well, it is simple, but it's not always easy. Sometimes ideas come up in the moment, sometimes they don't. Sometimes they come up when we don't think about it. But we do feel that the questions we ask ourselves matter. They shape what we give attention to. In a sense, they plant seeds and nurture them. And we get to choose which seeds we plant.'

Joseph: 'And here, these seeds become the food we're eating. Quite literally.'

Roberta, smirking: 'Ahh, nice analogy, Joseph. Didn't see that one coming.'

Joseph: 'I'm flattered.'

Everybody at the table chuckled and enjoyed the light-heartedness.

Sue: 'If I can add something to answer your question, Maryam, the ideas are born here, but they are just a starting point, a spark. Seeing it through and making them happen obviously requires effort, perseverance and patience. The initial ideas might not evolve, because either there are obstacles we didn't foresee or we are working to further improve on the idea. When something feels meaningful, when there's a sense of inspiration, in our experience it's usually been successful.'

Maryam: 'Why do you think that is?'

Sue: 'Well, for starters it's because there's enough energy in the team to make it happen. We find ways.'

Maryam: 'You're motivated?'

Sue: 'No, not quite. That's different. We feel energised. There is no motivation necessary. We do it for us.'

Ahmed: 'If I may jump in here, I think Sue is spot on. When what we're working on is meaningful to us – when it's a way of expressing what we deeply care about, sometimes for a reason we might not even fully understand – we seem to have an abundant energy to make it work. And, I have noticed that our customers feel this as well. Has anyone else noticed that?'

People around the table nodded while eating or taking a sip of water.

Ahmed: 'I don't know how to say this. It's not something we actually do, you know. It's just... the joy we sense in each of us and among us seems to rub off. And that, I think, makes the ideas successful. It's a self-fulfilling prophecy. Am I making any sense?'

Maryam: 'Yes, Ahmed, you are. I just didn't see it so clearly before you said it this way. When I come to the restaurant, I come because of all of you as well as the food. The food is great – it's yummy, it looks good, it's healthy, it's good quality, the price is right. But then, it wouldn't be the same if you just put it in a self-service counter and disappeared. This cinnamon dish, for example, is just a vehicle that transports your energy, a part of who you are. I'm buying you, your joy, what you stand for... not just a cinnamon roll.'

Ahmed, raising his eyebrows and winking: 'Well, now you know all of our secrets. But for the record, I'm not for sale.'

Joseph: 'No worries, Ahmed. We won't let you go.'

There was a moment of quiet. Everyone seemed to be focusing on their meal and simply enjoying the vibration of the conversation.

Deepa: 'There's one more way that coming from our sense of purpose helps us at times. We also use it as our north star for decision making, don't we?'

Sue: 'You're right. Keep going.'

Deepa: 'Well, for example, we used to sell sweets and fizzy drinks next to the checkout over there. During one of our meetings, Roberta brought out a book talking about the most recent research on sugar, its impact on health and ultimately on society. I think it was Joseph who then asked the question, "If we were to meet someone who says that he or she cares deeply about celebrating and nurturing the joy of life through great food and togetherness, would we expect that person to sell sugary drinks and sweets?"'

Maryam: 'That's a tough question to ask. I guess some of your customers would expect you to have the choices they want, right?'

Deepa: 'Indeed. It wasn't an easy discussion to have, but it was a necessary and valuable one. It wasn't a decision that could be made through logic alone. The only tangible data point we had was how much revenue we were making from those products. We realised that there was no way of telling how much revenue we would lose if we stopped selling them...'

Sue: '...or how much more revenue we would make because of that choice.'

Deepa: 'Indeed. It was a long debate that took place in meetings, and corridors, and inside of each of us, to be frank. Initially we spoke about values, such as freedom of choice versus responsibility for health. That didn't help. We were going round in circles. And then there came a point where we all realised this decision was not for our minds to make; it was a decision of the soul. In the end, we each asked ourselves, "How would I feel if we made that choice? Would I feel inspired to be part of what we were creating, or tense, or neutral?" We listened to what our hearts and bodies were telling us.'

Maryam: 'It looks like you made a choice.'

Roberta: 'Yes, we did, and I'm glad Paul supported it. We decided to stop selling products with large amounts of sugar, and products you wouldn't necessarily expect to contain sugar, such as crisps. Strangely, most of us had a sense of clarity once we'd made that choice.'

Maryam: 'And then what happened?'

Sue: 'Thanks for asking, because that was the part of the journey we learned the most from, I think. At least I did. Once we had decided to go ahead with our choice, we explained it to our customers, of course. We made an announcement on the app and put leaflets on the tables. A few of us went around to explain our rationale.

'We were overwhelmed by the reactions we got. There were a few people who seemed a bit disappointed at first, but a large majority of people told us how deeply they appreciated our care and thoughtfulness. Many felt supported in their desire to live a healthier lifestyle, especially during their work hours. And we started receiving requests to sell alternatives to sugary snacks and fizzy drinks. People sent us photos of products they loved. We had new customers coming in, and many existing customers came more often.'

Deepa: 'Bottom line is that our overall footfall increased, and our revenue with the new drinks and snacks went up over 10%. We didn't expect that.'

Ahmed: 'I've realised that so far, we've never regretted a decision we've made when we've felt moved or inspired. Of course, it needs to make sense as well, but that question is often merely the starting point and insufficient to bring clarity.'

Sue: 'I feel the same. By the way, the next thing we'll be doing is fasting week.'

Maryam was puzzled. 'What do you mean – no food? But wouldn't that defy the fundamental existence of a restaurant?'

Sue: 'At first sight, it might look that way. We will still offer food, for example light broths or juices that support a well-defined one-week fasting-programme. You see, many people don't have the time or energy to prepare particular food in the evenings and then put it into containers for the next day. Then they have no microwaves or plates in their offices. So, we'll take care of that. For us it's easy.'

Ahmed: 'Many of our customers have also shared with us that while they see the various mental and physical health benefits of fasting, they find it a bit daunting to do it on their own. There are quite a few who have never fasted before and are not sure how to approach it, so we thought that three or four times a year, we'd help our colleagues to do it together, follow the same plan, share experiences and encourage each other. We've even spoken with the medical team at HQ and they are happy to come along during lunch hours to provide fifteen-minute education boosters and answer questions. We will start officially announcing it next week, but the truth is, we already have over fifty people who would like to participate.'

Joseph: 'We feel this is a wonderful way of manifesting our purpose. In fact, as we have all learned more about fasting and experienced it ourselves, we've realised that we've become more appreciative of the food we're consuming. And that can only be helpful for us as a restaurant.'

Maryam: 'Thanks, everyone, for sharing these experiences and reflections with me. I'm so grateful for your openness. What you're saying relates to a conversation that Paul and I had a few weeks ago about who we are and how we might be guided by the wisdom of our soul. And while this has all started to make some sense to me, I have been wondering more and more how this awareness could help me in my business. Well, I believe you've just shared that path with me. Thank you.'

In this moment, everyone at the table felt a deep sense of connection with Maryam, as well as each other. It was peaceful and joyous.

Paul: 'I would love to share this. I recently discovered[8] that in ancient Chinese, the word for business is composed of two characters. The first one can be translated as "life", the second one is translated as "meaning". Over 3,000 years ago, our ancestors discovered that business is a way of giving meaning to our lives. When we allow ourselves to come from that place of inspiration, we both tap into our own energy sources and awaken those in others. It makes good business sense to me.'

Maryam, smiling at Paul: 'Looks like there were already a few Chief Energy Officers 3,000 years ago.'

Ahmed had brought coffee and tea over for everyone, along with a selection of the cinnamon cookies and desserts. He invited everyone to help themselves. Then Maryam looked around the table.

Maryam: 'So, what else would you say helps you to manage your energy in this team?'

Becoming net-positive

Joseph: 'Well, I don't know about the others, but I feel there's not so much a single thing I could point to. It's a mindset. When it comes to policies, procedures or investments, these are in our sphere of control or influence. We are aiming to be net-positive.'

Maryam: 'Net-positive? In what sense?'

Joseph: 'We believe that the things we do don't only cost and generate money. If we look at a decision purely this way, we're

---

8   *The Living Company*, Arie de Geus, Foreword by Peter Senge

missing the more fundamental source
of success of our business...'

Maryam: '... human energy.'

Joseph: 'So, we're asking ourselves
a simple question: "As a result of
doing things this way, would the
human energy available to us increase
or decrease?" In other words, do we gain
more human energy than we have to invest to do
things this way? Are we net-positive? And, of course, we don't really
mean the quantity but the quality of the energy. The frequency of the
vibration, if you like, needs to go up, or be stable at least.'

'As a result of
doing things this way,
would the human energy
increase or decrease?
Are we net-positive?'

Maryam: 'If not, it would probably be an unattractive business
case. I can see that. So, what are some examples of net-positive
policies?'

Roberta: 'I think, the way we have changed our work hours has
helped everyone here to be at our best more often. We have got
rid of the rigid start and end times – they created more frustration
than they helped. They created problems that we wouldn't have
had otherwise, and were merely a reflection of the belief that one
can't truly trust people to work the hours they've agreed upon. In
a sense, rigid hours assume that people will break their contracts
before they've even started working here. That's an implied judgment that limits everyone's energy.'

Deepa: 'It's also a reflection of the belief that performance is linear –
the more hours you put in, the more output you get. And we find
this is only partly true.'

Maryam: 'So, how do you organise your working hours then?'

Sue: 'We simply agree a number of work hours per year and per month. It's like an account, and the accounts are visible to everyone. We are mutually accountable to use our time in ways that help us to fulfil our mission and ensure we're all net-positive while doing so. We meet as a team every two weeks to plan how we can best balance different work and private needs. That's the human energy we invest in the process.

'Now, it's clear that we'll need all hands on deck during certain hours. And there are some limitations in terms of who can do what because of our different skills. That's a given. But then there are days, and times during the day, when we need fewer people.'

Ahmed: 'At the same time, we all have various physical, emotional and mental needs that help us to fuel our energy reservoirs. For example, I have a family karate class I'm attending with my son on Thursday afternoons. It really means a lot to me, because it's quality time with him and I work out at the same time. Joseph sometimes takes care of the kids on mornings or afternoons when his wife needs to travel for work, and so on.'

Deepa: 'Also, some things can only be done here on the ground, including cooking and receiving merchandise, or checking inventories. But then, Roberta – who is mostly the one who writes the menus and updates our app for the week – used to do that here using the office PC. She got up early to beat the traffic and have a bit of quiet time, but it was always stressful. Nowadays, she usually does it from home on her iPad in the morning. Then, when the traffic has calmed down, she goes to the market and joins us afterwards.'

Roberta: 'Yes, that helps a lot, and is less energy draining. It's important to see that our intention goes beyond mere flexibility to accommodate and organise work and home life, although that in itself helps to increase and replenish energy. What I mean is we're accepting that human energy is not linear. It goes up and down, sometimes for obvious reasons, and sometimes it just happens. So, when people feel a bit drained, we often encourage them to go home earlier or come in later and have a good night's sleep. If we can make it happen – and most of the time we can, we will.'

Paul: 'Thank you for highlighting that, Roberta. Allow me to add a little more here. The physical health that Roberta pointed out is vital from an energy perspective. For example, when we have low physical energy, our state of heart tends to be more closed as well. At least it's more fragile. When we're physically exhausted, our mind tends to produce less healthy thoughts that are reflected in our state of heart.'

Maryam: 'I've just realised why most of the arguments we have at home happen early in the morning or late in the evening. It's not because we don't see each other in between.'

Deepa: 'Looks like your family and mine have a lot in common.'

Everyone chuckled.

Paul, looking at Maryam: 'And I think there's one more dimension. You see, yesterday morning when we met outside, we touched upon the oneness of body and mind. And when we met at your home, we explored the power and value of listening to our intuition.'

Maryam: 'Yes.'

Paul: 'Now, how would you say we are able to listen to intuition? I mean practically, what do you listen to?'

Maryam and the team reflected.

Maryam: 'My heart...'

Paul: 'What else?'

Maryam: 'My breathing, my chest... how my body feels.'

Paul: 'You're listening to your body. You're listening with your body. Your body truly is an intuition machine. It senses things and communicates with you. And learning to listen to what it is saying opens a wide door to your intuition and innate wisdom. But it can't do the job so well when it's tired. In that case, you or I don't listen so well. So, to fully leverage the power of both our mind and our soul, we need to take care of our bodies. And our bodies need sleep and rest as much as tension and action.'

Maryam: 'Thank you, Paul, for highlighting that. And I can see more and more how the net-positive mindset helps you to translate some of the awareness of human energy sources into tangible actions and decisions. The examples you've mentioned make great sense. I guess, though, there must be quite a number things, like work hours, that neither you, Paul, nor the team can decide on your own?'

Sue: 'You're quite right. And in fact some of the things that work here don't make sense for other departments where people have different needs and constraints. That's why we prefer to come from universal mindsets and principles of human energy, rather than rules.'

Maryam: 'What's the difference for you?'

Sue: 'Well, for example, how we manage work hours here might be completely impractical or even counterproductive for other people. Yet the fundamental principles of our polices are net-positive when it comes to human energy and can inform better decisions elsewhere. We have regular conversations with our friends in the human resources department, and they've become real thinking partners over time. Nowadays we're not only talking about the support and approvals we need for adopting some of the policies here, we've also been asked to give input into new initiatives.'

Paul: 'Last week we shared our thoughts about the "Employee Promise", a document that captures what we as an organisation stand for and are committed to giving to our employees. Our Chief Executive Officer, Amy, would like it to become the guiding mission of all HR work across the organisation. Just as we work to fulfil our customer promise, she would like us to do the same for our employees. In the long run, she said we would develop a promise for other stakeholders, like suppliers and partners and the communities in which we live. I believe everyone here feels honoured that we've been invited to contribute to the development of this document.'

Maryam: 'I have no doubt about that, and I'm not surprised at all. I know it's a work in progress, but can you tell me a bit more about the Employee Promise?'

Paul: 'Well, it's fundamentally rooted in the understanding of the sources of energy you and I spoke about. It will be a commitment to support and treat our employees in such ways that acknowledge and systematically nurture their four energy sources: the heart, the mind, the body and the soul. Amy seems convinced that if we treat our employees really, really, really, really well by making their human energy our main point of reference, it will pay off and we will perform significantly better than our competition. In her view, that's because the value of all the assets we own is dependent on the human energy within our firm. It requires us to be more committed, intentional and systematic around awakening and nurturing human energy. Amy would like all of us to think and lead more often like Chief Energy Officers.'

Maryam: 'I find the mere intention inspiring and energising. So, what does she want to do with it?'

Roberta: 'I feel the same, Maryam. There's no other company I would rather like to work for, and I tell all my friends who work in our sector that if they can, they should join us.

'To answer your question – for a start, our Employee Promise will inform our priorities and investment choices in terms of how we help people develop and do even more meaningful work, how we take care of our colleagues so that they are healthy and genuinely enjoy being at work, how we help people supporting families, in particular children, and how we enable our employees to contribute to our communities and the environment in meaningful ways. Amy didn't use the term "net-positive", but essentially, that's what she wants us to become. After a year, she would like to start gathering regular feedback on how we're doing as a company with these promises, both to improve and learn, and to create awareness across the organisation.'

Maryam: 'That's a pretty bold yet inspiring goal, and there's a long way to go. But then, I guess that's exactly what bold, inspiring goals do – they set things in motion and channel energy in a purposeful direction.'

Paul: 'You're spot on, Maryam.'

Deepa: 'There is so much more that we could share with you, Maryam, but I guess we won't have time to share it all today. I think I can speak on behalf of everyone around the table when I say that we deeply appreciate your interest in our work, and you are always welcome to come along. The truth is we eat lunch every day...'

A gentle giggle went around the room.

Ahmed: 'Maybe next time I can show you our plans for the office refurbishment that I'm working on. It will have more daylight, quiet zones for reading and reflection. It will be decorated with personal objects that people bring in. That could fill one lunch alone.'

Sue: 'And we could talk about our thoughts around future mini-sabbatical arrangements, enabling those who want this to trade a part of their salary for taking a few consecutive weeks off.'

Joseph: 'We could also talk about the Master Chef trainings in Italy and France that we've designed to create a much more hands-on, rich and personal experience beyond the mere know-how in classrooms.'

Maryam: 'Wow! Team, I'm overwhelmed by your generosity. This was not only one of the yummiest lunches I've had this month, it was also one of the richest. My mind is full of ideas, my heart feels inspired, and I think I've just made some new friends. I will most certainly take you up on your invitation, and would like to extend that invitation to one of my offsite team meetings in the future. For us, it's a bit harder to have lunch together as we need a few flight-tickets, but when it happens, please come and join us. Paul, if it's OK with you, I'd like our teams to meet.'

Paul: 'Ahh, that would be wonderful. There's no convincing required.'

Coherence[9]

Joseph: 'Hey, before we all get on with our things, shall we do our usual 4-minute brain dessert?'

Everyone, except Maryam, nodded. 'Yeah sure, let's go,' someone said. Paul noticed Maryam's look, and realised she couldn't know what Joseph was referring to.

Paul: 'Maryam, this is just a very simple practice we typically start our days with, or often do together at the start or end of our meetings. As Joseph said, it literally takes a couple of minutes. Do you want to try it with us? Joseph will guide you.'

Maryam wasn't quite sure what to say, yet she was curious.

Maryam: 'Well, OK. I guess I like dessert.'

The team giggled and smiled at her.

Joseph: 'Excellent. You'll enjoy this. Just follow my guidance – I'll do it for everyone.'

Maryam: 'OK, let's go.'

Joseph: 'Alright, let's sit down comfortably, with our feet on the ground and our backs straight, just so we can breathe more easily.'

Joseph let everybody find a comfortable position.

Joseph: 'Maryam, if you want to close your eyes for this, go ahead. You don't have to, but I personally prefer closing my eyes. It helps me focus. And then, just breathe naturally and start with finding

9   The following section is based on the research and practices developed by the Heart-Math Institute: www.heartmath.com

your breath. There's nothing you need to do, just notice your breath...

...

breathing in, be aware you're breathing in

...

breathing out, be aware you're breathing out.'

Joseph allowed a few moments to become aware of the sensation of breathing, and then spoke with a gentle yet still very natural voice.

Joseph: 'OK, now, at the count of three, I'd like us to start breathing a little bit more deeply and in a very controlled... regular fashion. We will be breathing in for five seconds and breathing out for five seconds. And all you do then is maintain this regular breathing pattern.

Now... at the count of three, let's start... one... two... three.'

Now, Joseph only whispered.

Joseph: 'Breathe in...1... 2... 3... 4... 5

Breathe out...1... 2... 3... 4... 5

Breathe in... 1... 2... 3... 4... 5

Breathe out...1... 2... 3... 4... 5

Let's now carry on our own...'

Joseph remained quiet, breathing himself and allowing everyone else to get into the controlled breathing pattern.

Joseph: 'OK, that's wonderful. Please carry on, and enjoy your breathing and, if you like, feel free to gently smile at your breath – it keeps you alive.

...

Now that you're breathing in this regular fashion, I'd like you to focus on you heart space.

...

Imagine you're breathing *through* your heart... as if there was a large hole through which you can effortlessly breathe in... and breathe out. And simply carry on breathing... 5 counts in... 5 counts out...

... you're doing great, Maryam...'

Joseph let everyone focus on their heart for about a minute. He didn't need a watch. He knew a minute was up after six in and out breaths.

Joseph: 'OK, now that our hearts have started copying our breathing pattern, I'd like us to bring to mind someone towards whom we feel a deep sense of gratitude... or a situation or circumstance for which you feel profoundly grateful.

...

If it's a person, imagine that person is with you right now, sitting in front of you... maybe holding you.

...

Bring to mind the beautiful gifts they gave you in life... and... rather than thinking it... *feel* this sense of gratitude in your heart... allow it to fill your heart entirely.'

He waited a brief moment so that everyone could experience the feeling.

Joseph: 'OK, that's it. Thanks everyone for enjoying our dessert together, I'll see you around in the kitchen.'

Everyone stood up, shook hands or hugged, and quickly cleaned up the table together. Joseph turned to Maryam, who sat quietly.

Joseph: 'Just out of curiosity, Maryam – how are you feeling now?'

Maryam: 'Oh, what can I say? I feel... wonderful... light somehow... clear.'

Joseph: 'Ah, that's wonderful. I'm not surprised. You have more oxygen in your body than before, and eighty percent of that goes straight to your brain. Oxygen is a real treat for your brain.'

Maryam: 'Ah... the dessert, right?'

Joseph: 'Yes, that's part of the dish, the cake if you like. Plus, your heart is in a very powerful state right now, we call it 'coherence'. In such a state it's emitting certain neurotransmitters that allow your brain to operate much better and keep your body healthy.'

Maryam: '... the vanilla sauce for the cake?'

Joseph: 'Indeed, it's the topping. And the good news is it's free and has zero calories. You can do this as often as you like during the day. You can even do it with your eyes open in the middle of a meeting – and no one would even notice. And with a bit of practice the impact will grow even stronger.'

Maryam: 'Thank you, Joseph, for sharing this with me. It feels like another gift.'

Joseph: 'You're so welcome, Maryam. You're part of the team. I'll see you around.'

Maryam: 'See you...'Maryam waved goodbye, and Paul offered to accompany Maryam on her way back to the office.

It was a warm day and they could feel the energy of summer was claiming its place. Maryam and Paul stopped in the shadow of a tree.

Maryam: 'Paul, I'm intrigued. What just happened? I mean, what did we actually do? And why do I feel so elated. My state of heart is wide open. Joseph spoke about "coherence". Was does that mean?'

Paul: 'Ah, it's a great feeling isn't it? It's a simple and powerful practice that has helped me enormously, especially when faced with difficult situations and when my state of heart starts to close down. If you have a moment, I'll explain.'

Maryam: 'Yes please. I still have a few minutes.'

Paul: 'Well, let me back up. There's something you need to know about your heart that we haven't spoken about I think. You see, you heart is actually never beating at the same heart rate. Your heart rate is always changing. Right now it might be 80 beats per second, and now its 80 and a half. That constant change is called heart rate variability.'

Mariam: 'That sounds fancy.'

Paul smiled: 'It does. And what comes next has been life-changing for me, and has most certainty transformed how the team and I deal with strong emotions and even difficult decisions. There's research that suggests that there are two kinds of fundamental patterns our heart rate variability can take. When it's in a so-called state of *coherence* – that's what Joseph referred to – our heart rate increases for five seconds, and then goes down for five seconds. And so on.'

Paul grabbed a stick I found on the ground and drew a line in the sand...

Paul: 'If we measured your heart rate variability in a coherent state, it would look a bit like this.'

Maryam: 'That looks pretty smooth.'

Paul: 'Yes. Now, when our hearts are in a not-so-coherent state, when they are in an *incoherent* state, your heart rate variability starts looking a little bit more like this.'

Paul drew a second picture in the sand...

Maryam: 'Oh, that looks like it's in trouble a bit.'

Paul: 'You're spot on. In the long run, it is. And so is our brain. So, here's the next bit of what we know from science. When our hearts beat in such a coherent way, we tend to have more mental clarity and more perspective, and we find it easier to stay focused. We also tend to be more creative.'

Maryam: 'Oh, I want that! Sounds like a magic wand.'

Paul: 'Well it is, only that it's no magic – it's biology. Now, vice versa, it's also been proven that when our hearts are in more incoherent states, these capacities of ours are limited. There's more mental fuzziness, your thoughts are more scattered, and emotionally we tend to be more fragile. Have you ever been under time pressure frantically looking for your keys, yelling, only to find you've been holding them in your hand all the time?'

Maryam: 'Oh, I certainly know *that* feeling.'

Paul: 'Well, the chances are, your heart was in a state of incoherence.'

Maryam: 'Probably. Now, given that we do enter such states from time to time, how would I transform my heart rate variability from an incoherent into a more coherent state? I mean, that would be truly powerful, wouldn't it? But I'm not aware of a button I can press, right?'

Paul: 'Indeed, it's not under your direct control. It's your autonomous nervous system taking care of that for you. And it's pretty good at managing your heart.'

Maryam: 'Well, I guess then I could shift my thinking, as we said. Although...'

Paul: 'Although?'

Maryam: 'Well... any time I was in such a state and someone told me to "take it easy" or gave me some advice on how to "shift my thinking" it got me even more upset. And when I can't help do just that with others, I tend to get this angry look, if you see what I mean.'

Paul: 'Oh, I do. In fact, in such states our minds don't seem to be receptive for any healthy thinking. There's a little part in our brain, called the amygdala, whose job it is to scan our environment for danger. And when it thinks you're in a dangerous situation it puts you into a possibly lifesaving autopilot mode.'

Maryam: 'Also known as stress, right?'

Paul: 'Yes. That's what we call stress. And your body experiences that whether you want it or not. Now, because the amygdala's job is to keep you alive, it has evolved to be pretty fast. But it has traded that off for accuracy. To be on the safe side, so to say, it will opt for the alarm bell. So, while most situations nowadays are not truly life threatening, it will signal danger to your heart.'

Maryam: 'Like when someone's disagreeing with your point of view, or I'm worried about the outcome of a meeting?'

Paul: 'That's right, things of that nature. It doesn't matter if the threat is real. What matters is it's *perceived* as real. In fact, like in your second example, the situation doesn't even need to take place for the amygdala to qualify it as a threat. It's enough to imagine it. Now, unfortunately the amygdala doesn't seem to easily admit mistakes. It needs some time to admit. And until that happens, if it happens, your brain is in a kind of "amygdala hijack".'

Maryam: 'Oh, I like that. The amygdala is in charge, and I can't reason with the amygdala.'

Paul: 'Indeed, it doesn't understand language. Or, in other words, it's hard to talk yourself out of a closed state of heart. Yet, because our body and mind are one, there's a different door we can take.'

Maryam: 'So, changing my thinking might be futile in this moment, nor I can change my heart rate variability directly neither. What's left?'

Paul: Breath. 'It's your gateway to peace. It's the magic wand you mentioned.'

Maryam: 'Why breath? Why is it a gateway?'

Paul: 'Well, for two reasons. Would you say you can control your breathing if you want to?'

Maryam: 'Hmm, yes. I can choose to breathe slow and fast, deep or shallow.'

Paul: 'Indeed. Now, here comes the magic – when we breathe in, our heart beat goes up. And when we breathe out, our heart beat goes down. Every time.'

Maryam: 'That is something I wasn't aware of. So, when I breathe in for 5 seconds, and breathe out for 5 seconds and continue doing that, then...'

Paul: '... then your heart beat starts to emulate that very pattern. It becomes coherent.'

Maryam: 'Wow. That means that I actually *can* impact my heart rate variability.'

Paul: 'Yes you can. And here comes the second part of the magic. When your heart is beating this way the amygdala releases, so to speak, the kidnapped mind. When the heart beats this way, the amygdala knows, if you like, it can't be a threat. The heart communicates with the mind.'

Maryam: 'That's fascinating. So in this case, my body, I mean my heart, takes the lead.'

Paul: 'Very much so. And... now that your mind is free again, it can engage in healthy thinking.'

Maryam: 'Now I can focus my mind on what I choose, like thoughts of gratitude.'

Paul: 'Yes, now it has access again to its full capacity. It is capable to produce and focus on healthy powerful thoughts, such as gratitude. And what do healthy thoughts do with our state of heart?'

Maryam: 'They open it up.'

Paul: 'They do. And that's not only a metaphor. It's actually happening at a molecular level. In fact, your heart is much more than a muscle moving your blood, albeit that alone is already a wonder in itself. It is also a gland.'

Maryam: 'What does that mean?'

Paul: 'It means that some very important neurochemicals, such as norepinephrine, dopamine and in particular serotonin, that affect our mood and social behaviour, are actually created in the heart itself. It's the *heart* that produces the very chemical ingredients we need for healthy high performance as individuals, as teams, as organisations. And some, like serotonin, go straight to the brain.'

Mariam: 'Wow, so, physically, we cannot truly perform with a closed state of heart.'

Paul: 'And vice versa, once we think appreciative, grateful thoughts, and experience appreciative grateful feelings as a result, our hearts produce more of these ingredients. It's an infinite source of energy.'

Maryam: 'That's why Joseph asked us to focus on something we're feeling grateful for, right?'

Paul: 'Yes, energy truly goes where thought goes. It's not only a metaphor. It happens in a quite material sense.'

Maryam was excited. She paused to allow and enjoy her understanding to unfold... then she had to smile.

Maryam: 'It's the heart! Paul, imagine... imagine if the majority of our five thousand colleagues just spent 10% less time in an amygdala hijack. Imagine then that 10% more time that the five thousand hearts in our company would be busy producing serotonin.'

Paul: 'Yes?'

Maryam: 'It would change everything. I mean – everything. We'd have almost infinitely more power. At no cost.'

Paul: 'Yes.'

Maryam gazed at the two pictures Paul had drawn into the sand in front of them.

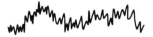   

Paul: '... you're thinking. What do you see?'

Maryam: 'Well, I was wondering how I can know the state of my heart rate variability. You see, I'm not sure if I'd like to wear a heart rate monitor throughout the day to be aware. And then it just occurred to me that I have a built-in heart rate variability monitor.'

Paul: 'And what is that?'

Maryam completed Paul's images...

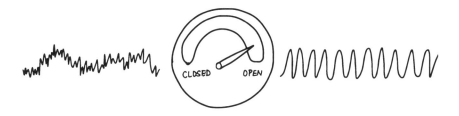

Maryam: 'My state of heart. When I'm mindful of my state of heart, I just know what's going on.'

Paul smiled at her and didn't say anything.

Embodying Humanity

Maryam: 'Paul, I would like to thank you. I feel blessed by your friendship, your generosity and the moments of reflection and joy we have had together. Thank you for inviting me to meet some of your team, I found it energising to listen to them.'

She paused, and Paul silently let her find her thoughts.

Maryam: 'You see, I always knew, of course, that being a general manager of any kind is about people. But this was merely an intellectual understanding. Even then, I was often cynical. Now... I can *feel* it. Not so much because of the content of our conversations, but because of your presence. I'm not sure if this makes sense. I don't quite understand why, but although I have as many issues to tackle as I did two months ago, I feel more... peaceful. I don't know how else to describe it.'

Paul didn't respond. Both spontaneously grabbed each other's hands and pressed them together gently as if to say thank you to each other. Both knew that their silence expressed how they felt more truly than any words they could have chosen to speak.

Paul: 'Maryam – what a wonderful insight you just shared with me. We've spoken about many aspects of leadership, and what we can do as leaders to awaken, nurture and channel energy in others and ourselves. And while mindfulness of our state of heart and thought process is important, as well as compassionate, non-dualistic thinking, listening and talking, practising our capacity to forgive and let go, and the policies and office designs we create, it is not really the intellectual description or understanding of these components that is going to nurture more loving energies in our teams and organisations. Information doesn't transform us. How can you possibly discover what comes before thought through thought? That is the mystery of leadership.'

'How can you discover what comes before thought through thought? That is the mystery of leadership.'

Maryam: 'So it is the *experience* of these principles in others and ourselves that truly transforms us. I have experienced it in you and your team.'

Paul: 'Maybe the most transformative of all human experiences is the experience of each other's humanity. It seems to me that we become instantly more loving and compassionate in the presence of someone who allows him or herself to be human. It rubs off on us, because we're all connected. Our state of heart is infectious. That's the true power we have.'

Maryam: 'Then that would mean that my mere presence could transform people?'

Paul: 'I have no doubt that your loving human presence deeply affects other people – as long as you're not attached to transforming others. But don't take my word for it. Experience it.'

Maryam: 'Hmm, in the past, I was always looking for workshops, training, techniques or books to help me improve the state of heart and performance of my team. I knew I needed to be a role model, that's a no-brainer. But I didn't think of my mere presence as the catalyst for change.'

Paul: 'Maryam, there's nothing wrong with that. In a sense, workshops, techniques or books are like a great sheet of music written by an experienced composer. The musician will start by choosing and practising the notes that capture their sense of personal inspiration and experience. But it's only in the moment when they play in the presence of an audience and express themselves through the music that it touches the hearts of others. It's the presence of the musician playing music that transforms the energy in the room, not the music sheet. Even if the musician is the composer, we're paying for their presence and energy, not for the sound. We can download that. Our hearts will open, the energy shifts, if the music is truly meaningful to the musician,

'The most transformative of all human experiences is the experience of each other's humanity.'

an expression of their and our humanity. That is the spirit of performance.'

Maryam: 'Could it be that the only real obstacle to more loving leadership and organisations is that we simply lose touch with our humanity at times?'

Paul paused and reflected.

Paul: 'Let me share something that happened to me a few days after I came to your house. My friend Thomas, who runs the restaurant for one of our major suppliers, invited me to share our experiences with him and his team. We decided to gather in a nearby hotel to distance ourselves from our usual environment. And to make sure that everything ran smoothly, I decided to arrive the evening before, on a Sunday night. I didn't want to disappoint anyone, and although it wasn't far away, I felt nervous about being stuck in morning traffic.

'On that Sunday, I was invited to celebrate my niece's birthday, and she begged me to stay for dinner. Of course I stayed – I wanted to, although I felt a bit tense with regards to the time I had left to prepare the workshop room. I don't do that sort of thing every day.

'It was already 9.30pm when I arrived at the hotel, and almost 10pm when I got to the room. Now, I had shared with the hotel manager that all they needed to do was set up the room. Thomas had even sent some of the things we would need two weeks earlier. But when I got to the room, nothing was the way I expected it to be. The room was too small, the set-up was not professional, there was no projector ready to go, and the things Thomas had sent weren't there. Clearly something had been lost in communication.

'I felt disappointed and anxious I wouldn't be able to get ready in time, or I'd have to sacrifice a good night's sleep to do so. I couldn't find any hotel employees to help, so I went back to the receptionist to ask for the banquet manager.

'He arrived fifteen minutes later – it must have been 10.30pm by then. I explained what I had expected and that I needed to go to bed with some peace of mind. I hoped that he would simply help me to set up the room; I thought we could be ready in fifteen minutes. Instead he became defensive. He explained to me that he was unable to help because the hotel had changed the room at the last minute. He then said his shift was over and he would take care of it first thing in the morning.

'That's when I snapped. My heart closed. I gave him a lecture on customer service, and what would happen at my restaurant if I took a similar attitude and approach. Of course, this was a waste of breath. He became even more defensive and found even more reasons why things were as they were. My heart was thumping. I was angry, and I must have been quite intimidating. And in the moment, I felt that was justified.'

Maryam: 'I had no idea you could be this way.'

Paul: 'Together with the general manager, who as luck would have it was still around, we were able to find a better room and ensure that everything would be ready in time for the next morning. But the next day, I could sense the friction between the banquet manager and me. It felt strange to talk with the team in front of me about the Chief Energy Officer mindset when he was around during the breaks.

'During lunch break, I excused myself and took a walk outside to find some quiet. I sat on a bench and quietened down, becoming aware of my feelings. With a bit of distance, I replayed the previous evening. I was wondering how I had been able to feel and act the way I had. If someone had asked me how I felt while acting that way, what would I have told them?

'As I reflected, I realised I would have said that I can treat my fellow humans with unkindness and hurt them in moments when I feel unsafe or overwhelmed myself – the times when I sense that something is out of my control. Being unkind then creates the illusion in me that I am superior, and I secretly want this superiority to make me feel safe and in control again. When I'm feeling irritated by the actions of others, I'm looking at the areas of my own growth I haven't fully accepted yet.'

Maryam: 'What did you do then?'

Paul: 'I went to see the banquet manager, Garry, and asked if he had a moment. It was obvious how uncomfortable he felt. I told him, "I'm sorry for my tone and how I spoke to you yesterday." He replied that it was OK and that the hotel hadn't provided the service I'd expected. I shared with him that while that was probably the case, it was still my choice to be unkind to him, and I asked him to forgive me for hurting him.'

Maryam: 'How did he react?'

Paul: 'He was moved. He talked about his day and his experience of working at the hotel so far. Then we talked about family and life more broadly. The whole energy changed. I asked him if he'd be willing to join me in the afternoon to share our experiences between yesterday evening and now. He accepted. It was such a wonderful moment for everyone, a very human moment.'

Maryam: 'I can imagine. Thank you for sharing this, Paul. So, are you saying that an obstacle to more loving leadership is that we can lose sight of our humanity at times?'

Paul: 'Not quite. Becoming more loving and compassionate is probably the destination for us humans, but the reason we're here is to practise, not to be perfect. Our human imperfections – our fear, anger, irritation, resentment – are the practice, like in the instance with Garry. While unnecessary, they seem necessary for us to become aware of the illusion of scarcity and our attachments that nurture our fears. When we look into these feelings, they help us develop compassion for fellow human beings who feel the same, so we can experience how we return to love more often, many times during our days. It's the full experience of humanity that nurtures love. When we exclude the parts we don't like, we can't grow.'

Maryam gave Paul a hug, and then they both returned to work. When she arrived at her office, she took out her notebook, looked at an empty page, and wrote down a sentence that came from her heart.

Humanity is the source, goal and path of true leadership.

Journaling

Maryam went to bed early and experienced a deep, peaceful sleep. The next morning, after her meditation practice and before heading for the office, she took a brief moment to jot down the thoughts, insights and questions that emerged from the meeting with Paul's team and their conversation.

- It's the heart – stupid!

- Everything is connected. The circle of energy works both ways... from thought to body (action) and from body to thought. Our thoughts impact our state of heart and our behaviours. At the same time our breath can help us stay in an open state of heart and keep perspective.

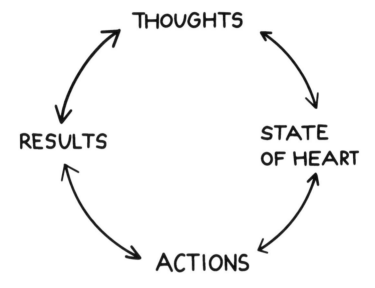

- Maybe... our thoughts and our breath are the only two forms of human energy I can truly control:

  » Let's start our meetings with a coherence breathing moment.

  » I can use my state of heart to 'monitor' my coherence levels throughout the day. I can engage in coherence breathing anytime, also in the middle of a meeting or a conversation.

  » Energy goes where thought goes.

- Are our processes and policies 'net-positive'? Let us be guided by that question.

- Decision making:

- » I can use the wisdom of my heart by asking: how does it feel?

- » I can use the wisdom of my soul by asking: do I feel inspired?

- Purpose is a business-word for soul:

  - » Meaning is the gateway for purpose, inspiration our compass on the way

  - » Purpose is the fourth gateway of energy

What else can I do today to create a truly human organisation?

Epilogue

'And now here is my secret, a very simple secret:
It is only with the heart that one can see rightly;
what is essential is invisible to the eye.'

Antoine de Saint-Exupéry, The Little Prince

'Love comes more naturally to the
human heart than its opposite.'

Nelson Mandela

A few weeks later, Maryam went to the company restaurant with a new colleague, Ian, who had joined her team the previous week. Maryam had participated in the fasting week, and now felt both energised and renewed, yet she was also eager for Ian to try some 'soul food', as she referred to the restaurant team's menu.

Ian had a hard time choosing. 'Wow, this all looks great – if I could, I'd taste all of it.'

Joseph was standing nearby and overheard Ian's comment.

'Well, sir, why don't you do that then? If you like, I can create a tasting platter for you with a few of the highlights of today. Would that help you?'

Ian was touched by Joseph's mindfulness and care. He and Maryam sat down and enjoyed their food, learning about each other and talking about work.

Then, all of a sudden, Ian paused. 'I'm sorry, Maryam, I'm just stunned by the energy in this restaurant. It's everywhere… in the room, in the people. The food is awesome. I didn't expect this at all.'

Maryam: 'I know. That's why I wanted us to eat here today.'

Ian: 'I'm wondering how they do it. I would be very happy if I could create just some of this vibration in my own team.'

Maryam: 'Well, I guess you will need to become a Chief Energy Officer.'

Ian: 'Oh, that's a first. What does it mean?'

Maryam: 'We'll have to meet more often to answer that question. But for starters, have you ever…'

Chief Energy Officer Books

If as a result of experiencing Paul and Maryam's conversations you would like to continue exploring a theme that resonated with you, I've assembled a list of authors and their books that all have one thing in common: they have all inspired me in different ways, and accompanied me on my ongoing journey. This book would not be as it is today if any of these authors had not chosen to share their voices.

I believe some of these books can support you too as you continue your journey as Chief Energy Officer – at work, at home and in life. This list is in no way exhaustive. It simply represents a selection of some of the most gifted singers in this beautiful choir, to which I humbly add my voice.

In my view all these books offer profound and complementing perspectives allowing us to learn about energy – its nature, its sources, and how we nurture, transform and direct it in ourselves and in our organisations. Some also include the scientific research underpinning the views expressed in this book.

My separation into the sections below doesn't do any justice to the wisdom of these books; in fact most of them could be simultaneously in all sections. I still hope my structure helps you navigate and possibly find a few books that will become precious companions on your Chief Energy Officer path. A path with many beginnings and no endings.

The Role and Sources of Energy in Leadership

Servant Leadership: A Journey into the Nature of Legitimate Power and Greatness, by Robert K. Greenleaf and Larry C. Spears (1977, Paulist Press, Mahwah, NJ)

Humble Leadership: The Power of Relationships, Openness, and Trust, by Edgar H. Schein and Peter A. Schein (2018, Berrett-Koehler Publishers, Oakland, CA)

Winning from Within: A Breakthrough Method for Leading, Living, and Lasting Change, by Erica Ariel Fox (2013, Harper Business, New York, NY)

The Way We're Working Isn't Working: The Four Forgotten Needs That Energize Great Performance, by Tony Schwartz, Founder & CEO of The Energy Project (2010, The Free Press, New York, NY)

Drive: The Surprising Truth About What Motivates Us, by Daniel H. Pink (2019, Riverhead Books, New York, NY)

Altered Traits: Science Reveals How Meditation Changes Your Mind, Brain, and Body by Daniel Goleman and Richard J. Davidson (2017, Penguin, New York, NY)

Stealing Fire: How Silicon Valley, the Navy SEALs, and Maverick Scientists Are Revolutionizing the Way We Live and Work, by Steven Kotler and Jamie Wheal (2017, Harper Collins, New York, NY)

Heart and Mind: The Gateway of Thoughts, Feelings and Mindfulness

The Mood Elevator: Take Charge of Your Feelings, Become a Better You, By Larry Senn (2017, Berrett-Koehler Publishers, Oakland, CA)

Mindset: Changing The Way You think To Fulfil Your Potential, by Carol Dweck (2017, Robinson, London, Great Britain)

Cure: A Journey into the Science of Mind Over Body, by Jo Marchant (2017, Canongate Books, Edinburgh, Great Britain)

Leading with Questions: How Leaders Find the Right Solutions by Knowing What to Ask, by Michael J. Marquardt (2014, John Wiley and Sons, San Francisco, CA)

How to Fight, by Thich Nhat Hanh (2017, Parallax Press, Berkeley, CA)

Tribal Leadership: Leveraging Natural Groups to Build a Thriving Organization, by Dave Logan, John King, Halee Fischer-Wright (2018, HarperCollins, New York, NY)

Pivoting: A Coach's Guide to Igniting Substantial Change, by Ann L. Clancy, Jacqueline Binkert (2017, Palgrave Macmillan, New York, NY)

Creative Visualization: Use the Power of Your Imagination to Create What You Want in Your Life, by Shakti Gawain and Marci Shimoff (2002, Nataraj Publishing, Novato, CA)

Conscious You: Become The Hero of Your Own Story, by Nadjeschda Taranczewski (2018, Rethink Press, Great Britain)

Unlocking Leadership Mindtraps: How to Thrive in Complexity, by Jennifer Garvey Berger (2019, Stanford University Press, Stanford, CA)

Quantum Skills for Coaches: A Handbook for working with Energy and the Body-Mind in Coaching by Anette Simmons (2008, Word4Word, Great Britain)

The Fifth Discipline: The Art & Practice of The Learning Organization, by Peter M. Senge (2006, Doubleday, USA)

Soul: The Gateway of Consciousness and Purpose

Man's Search for Meaning, by Victor Frankl (2006, Beacon Press, Boston, MA)

The Secrets of the Bulletproof Spirit: How to Bounce Back from Life's Hardest Hits, by Azim Khamisa and Jillian Quinn (2018, Waterside Press, Cardiff, CA)

The Untethered Soul: The Journey Beyond Yourself, by Michael A. Singer (2017, New Harbinger Publications, Oakland, CA)

Start with Why: How Great Leaders Inspire Everyone to Take Action, by Simon Sinek (2009, Penguin Books, Great Britain)

The Enlightened Gardener, by Sydney Banks (2016, Lone Pine Publishing, Unites States)

Falling Upward: A Spirituality for the Two Halves of Life, by Richard Rohr (2011, Jossey-Bass, San Francisco, CA)

Love Is Letting Go of Fear, by Gerald G. Jampolsky (2011, Celestial Arts, New York, NY)

Power vs. Force, by David R. Hawkins (2012, Hay House, Carlsbad, CA)

Body: The Gateway of Doing and Being

Reinventing Organizations, by Frederic Laloux and Ken Wilber (2014, Nelson Parker, Shrewsbury, MA)

One-Moment Meditation: Stillness for People on the Go, by Martin Boroson (2019, Winter Road Publishing, Port Jefferson Station, NY)

The HeartMath Solution: The Institute of HeartMath's Revolutionary Program for Engaging the Power of the Heart's Intelligence, by Doc Lew Childre and Howard Martin (1999, HarperCollins, New York, NY)

Firms of Endearment: How World-Class Companies Profit from Passion and Purpose, by Rajendra Sisodia, Jagdish N. Sheth (2014, Pearson Education, Upper Saddle River, New Jersey)

Time to Think: Listening to Ignite the Human Mind, by Nancy Kline (1999, Hachette, Great Britain)

The Art of Gathering: How We Meet and Why It Matters, by Priya Parker (2018, Riverhead Books, New York, NY)

Physical Intelligence, by Patricia Peyton and Claire Dale (2019, Simon & Schuster, Great Britain)

Acknowledgements

I'd like to say that I feel truly grateful for everyone I've met and spent time with on my journey so far. And that includes people who might have made the circumstances of my life more challenging than I would have wanted them to be, along with those who have nurtured, cared for and loved me. I would not be who I am nor see the world as I do now if I hadn't met all of you, and this book would certainly not be what it has become. This is not *my* book; I've just written it to share what I can see up to now as a result of the life I've experienced so far, and – who knows – maybe even before that.

There are, of course, people who have had or continue to have a huge impact on my life, and as a consequence, on this book. Let me highlight a few.

After spending almost ten years working with Senn Delaney, I am not surprised that the team and spirit of this special organisation have become my alma mater. And this book cannot be truly separated from my ongoing journey with this very special organisation and its people. The book has been inspired by and rooted in the work we've done and continue doing, which has positively influenced the lives and work of so many, including myself.

I would like this book to be seen as a contribution to the important work of organisational consciousness, honouring its roots and nurturing it by both making connections and looking at it differently. Amy Turner, Sarah van der Burgh, Dustin Seale, Ian Johnston, Jim Hart, Nick Neuhausel, Laura Basha, Dianna Ott and Larry Senn: all of you, and many other team members, have sometimes directly, sometimes indirectly contributed to me finding and continuing my path. I've learned from your perspectives, your energy and actions. As such, your spirit and wisdom are in this book.

Amy, I feel particularly grateful for your friendship and advice over the years, which have always come from a place of genuine care and openness. You bring out the best in me and are indulgent with the rest. Your faith in me is in this book; the title was born from a conversation in Dubai when all you did was listen.

And then there is Paul Nakai. You are yet another wonderful gift in my life. And you know very well that this book would not exist if you hadn't asked me that day in San Francisco, 'What do you think about us connecting over the phone more regularly...?' That was more than ten years ago, and since then I've looked forward to each conversation, all starting with an affectionate, 'How are you, my dear friend...?' This book is a homage to your friendship and the unconditional love that you bring to me and many others. Thank you for walking with me. I thought we only made friends when we were young. Little did I know.

This book would not exist without the encouragement, advice, feedback and guidance of Azim Khamisa. Azim, you have become both a spiritual teacher and friend, and were the first one to read an early version of the manuscript. When we met in Dubai and I asked for your view, you not only encouraged me to finish the book as you felt it was important for me to do so, you also gave me a piece of advice at the right time:

'Don't hold back!' I hope that I haven't.

You then gave me back a version of the manuscript full of notes, observations and suggestions that I found to be invaluable. Thank you for being so generous with your time and love. Your insights and life experience, in particular but not only in the realm of forgiveness and consciousness, have found their way into and shaped this book. Last but not least, I'm grateful for what I've learned from you about the process of writing and publishing, which gave me perspective and hope.

I'd also like to thank Ann Clancy from the bottom of my heart. Ann, you have been a mentor to me in the realm of 'appreciative coaching'. The truth is, you too have walked with me a long way, and I couldn't imagine a world without you. Just as with Azim, your feedback and reflections on the early manuscript were both precious and encouraging. You've helped me realise that 'building bridges' is something I can't *not* do. And here we are. Thank you, my friend.

One day, I said, 'Hmm, wouldn't it be great if the book was illustrated?' I felt that images would offer another dimension and make the experience of reading even richer; I just didn't know anyone who would be capable, let alone willing to do this.

The next day, I stood in front of Anu Chacko's desk. We were colleagues at the time, but we didn't know each other well – yet. As I stood next to her, I noticed the sketches and drawings on her desk and I loved them immediately. And I'm sure you can guess what happened, given you're holding the result in your hand.

I asked Anu if she would consider illustrating a book that I had started writing. I said I couldn't promise it would ever get published, and that for now it was only a work in progress. Never will I forget her reaction. Looking at me with wet eyes, she said that she would feel humbled if we were to do this together. I subsequently discovered that Anu is a genuine artist, experimenting with various techniques and styles as ways to express what cannot be said in words so easily.

Anu, I've learned so much with and from you. Thank you for bringing your soul to this book, for taking a huge leap of faith. You have done far more than 'colouring thoughts'; your images have themselves triggered new thoughts that would not have been there without you. Thank you for your friendship, my dear sister.

I cannot close without thanking my wife and two children. Whatever I say here won't do their contribution and my infinite gratitude justice. The majority of the book was written while I was far away in Dubai. While we were separated, I used the gift of uninterrupted quietude to allow my thoughts to flow and give our separation a purpose. How often did I wish I could hug you? You always had faith in me.

And then, of course, my personal experiences as husband and father have informed the content of this book hugely. I grow with you, discover through you. I'm learning every day what love means because of you. I have no doubt that the world we want starts with our families, at home. And you help me see that. I love you.

I'd like to thank my parents who both, in their unique ways, taught me love. You allowed me to be here today. I love you, too.

And finally, I'd like to thank you, the reader, for choosing this book out of the many you could have chosen. It is merely a reflection of my own current consciousness, of what I'm able to 'see' right now. I truly hope it will be of value, helping you live the life you want and build organisations that contribute to the higher good of humankind and the planet. One more thought...

Some of the people who kindly offered to read the manuscript for this book have asked me if I made a conscious choice to use the names Maryam and Paul. The answer is yes and no. Of course, they could have had any names, but through the process of writing, I've become quite attached to both.

And both represent bridges. Maryam, for example, is a name that exists in Christian, Jewish and Muslim scriptures and is used across these and other cultures. While I could say a lot more about Maryam and what she stands for, she is in my eyes a reminder of what we all have in common. And one could see her as a connection between the intangible (soul) and the tangible (body).

The apostle Paul was one of the most prominent epitomes of human transformation. His life reminds us that transformation and peace are always possible, regardless of our past, regardless of our circumstances.

At the same time, Paul is a homage to Paul Sewell, who drove me to my hotel that momentous day and first encouraged me to write, and my dear friend Paul Nakai, without whom this book would most certainly not exist.

The Author

What gives Boris a heartfelt sense of meaning in life is to serve and witness leaders nurture and connect with higher forms of energy in themselves, their teams and organisations.

Boris has over 15 years of professional experience in organisation-wide culture-shaping, leadership development and personal transformation, and has been a Vice President with Senn Delaney, a Heidrick & Struggles company and culture-shaping pioneer, for over seven years. As a consultant, facilitator and coach, he has supported senior leaders to nurture more thriving organisational cultures at Rolls Royce, eBay, NATO, Majid Al Futtaim, ITT, Nomad Foods, Hertz, L'Occitane en Provence, Novartis and British Telecom. He co-devised and piloted the first ever Executive Development Programme in NATO. Prior to his work as a consultant Boris was responsible for the Leadership Development activities at a global division at Siemens.

On his journey Boris has worked with executives and employees at all levels in Europe, the Middle East, the United States, South America, Africa and Asia. Boris studied Economics in Toulouse, France and graduated from ESCP Europe following studies of international management in Paris, Oxford and Berlin. He is a certified coach, and a guest faculty member of the Middle East Leadership Academy (MELA), a non-profit organisation supporting high-potential business leaders to be catalysts for positive change.

Boris lives with his wife and two children in southern Germany. For many years he has also lived and worked in London, Genoa and Dubai. He is a passionate photographer with a desire to capture and show the light in everyone, and plays a bit of piano to entertain family and friends when he finds a good enough excuse to do so.

✉ boris@borisdiekmann.com
🔗 www.linkedin.com/in/borisdiekmann

Printed in Poland
by Amazon Fulfillment
Poland Sp. z o.o., Wrocław

90727756R00168